'An invaluable guide to a fine,
setting his life and music into t
Dodgson was not only a compos
caster on music, and the talks th
thousands of listeners to Radio 3. The music likewise, so it is not
surprising that the two pre-eminent guitarists of their day, Julian
Bream and John Williams, revelled in its élan and understanding of
the instrument. But as this book reveals, there is so much more to
savour and these pages rekindle a hunger to do so.'

Michael Berkeley, composer and broadcaster

'This wonderful collection of essays, interviews and personal reflections on Stephen Dodgson's life and music is utterly absorbing and
makes one want to delve deep into the many superb recordings of his
compositions. The combination of words from Dodgson's own pen
(and radio mic), descriptions of his music from the (always eminent)
performers who championed his music and musicological analysis
paints a vivid picture of a congenial and intellectual man who truly
valued the craft of composition and was capable of writing idiomatically for the most challenging collections of instruments. A valuable
resource for scholars and the general reader alike, I would heartily
recommend this book to composition students: much is to be learned
from Dodgson's attitude and approach over his long, illustrious career.'

Cheryl Frances-Hoad, composer

'Stephen Dodgson's ideas in music have always spoken to me directly,
as though written for my own ears, and they come directly from him,
pure and unobstructed by any superfluous or gratuitous colourings. I
think that that transparency, integrity and honesty are a constant in his
music. Like a burst of freshness, like a sunny afternoon, like the man
himself, full of fun, full of humour... and depth. So it's wonderful to
see this rich centenary collection where Stephen himself speaks from
the page, along with the many special photos throughout his life and
the recollections from fellow musicians and friends, reflecting on
Stephen the man and the musician – his generosity, his boundless
energy and that ever-present sense of fun and humour so clearly
brought to life.'

Paco Peña, guitarist

'A fascinating collection of writings about a man very much in the thick of musical life in Britain throughout his long composing career. Its aims are wide-ranging, attempting to place Stephen Dodgson in a historical context, offering biographical details of his life, testimonials from friends or admirers, and essays discussing his contribution as a composer to various musical genres. And the wonderfully reproduced photographs help to bring this clearly loveable and fun-loving man to life.

The result of a huge collaboration, the book's eclecticism and many-voiced discourse feels like a very true reflection of Stephen's own musical language, and of his willingness to turn his hand to almost anything. I cannot think there would be many composers for whom such a book would contain chapters devoted to music for harp, for guitar and for harpsichord! The love that the contributors bear for him and his music shines through the text, and helps to celebrate the vivid liveliness of Stephen's writing. A fine tribute to mark the centenary of the birth of a significant figure in the world of British Music.'

James Gilchrist, tenor

'Many fine 20th-century British composers are becoming neglected, as Thomas Hyde reminds us in his eloquent introduction to this centenary tribute to Stephen Dodgson. Best known today for his masterly guitar music, Stephen Dodgson did not adopt the radical modernism of many of his contemporaries. Instead, he wrote over 250 pieces of music in almost all genres, all of which are friendly to both players and listeners. 'My whole desire is for something positive, outgoing and full of life and motion', Dodgson so accurately said in an interview included in this excellent, comprehensive book, full of charming photographs, which must surely help revive his reputation.'

David Matthews, composer

BORN BY THE THAMES

Stephen Dodgson

A Centenary Celebration

EDITED BY OLIVER CHANDLER & THOMAS HYDE

de la Porte
PUBLISHING

de la Porte
PUBLISHING

First edition published in 2024 in Great Britain by
de la Porte Publishing
www.delaPortePublishing.co.uk

ISBN 978-1-8383269-1-3

10 9 8 7 6 5 4 3 2 1

A CIP catalogue record for this title
is available from the British Library.

Text design and typesetting by Typo•glyphix, Burton-on-Trent
Production editor: Leonora Dawson-Bowling
Indexer: Paula Clarke Bain

Printed and bound in Great Britain by CPI Books.

CONTENTS

INTRODUCTION

What to Do with a 1920s Boy?

THOMAS HYDE

One by one they reach their centenaries. And the British 1920s boys must be wondering whether they will *ever* get a moment in the limelight. For even in life, they were a generation of British composers in a frustrating no-man's land, stuck between the era of Walton and Tippett, both of whom got at least some of their scores at one time or another into the major international repertoire, and a younger generation of Birtwistle and Maxwell Davies who engaged with European modernism in intriguing and at times flamboyant ways. The 1920s boys were trapped by being neither one thing nor another. And has anything changed?

They were considered too advanced harmonically and too chromatic melodically to appeal to a wide musical public still wedded to Romanticism and who had at first even struggled with Walton ('such appalling discords, my dear, no melody at all' as the epigraph from Terence Rattigan's 'Aunt Edna' puts it[1]). But as they reached their maturities in the 1950s they could also be dismissed as too conservative, too insular by younger musicians excited at the advances of continental modernism in France and Germany. Even those who rejected a studiously constructed English pastoralism and folk-derived melodic language, à la Finzi and Vaughan Williams, found that an idiom derived

---

1 Terence Rattigan, *Collected Plays*, Vol.1 (Hamish Hamilton, 1953), p. xii.

from Bartók, Schoenberg and Hindemith seemed tame and worn out compared to what the European 1920s boys – Boulez, Henze and Stockhausen – were up to. Indeed, for many who followed them, these 1920s composers seemed English, but only in a non-exciting way: which is to say, by default for not being anything else. No, they were not cowpat, but there was still too much the atmosphere of the bowler hat.

Was it their education that was a problem? The 1930s boys would nearly all study abroad after graduating: Alexander Goehr with Messiaen in Paris, Nicholas Maw with Boulanger, Maxwell Davies with Petrassi in Rome, John McCabe in Munich. If the 1920s boys – or at least those born in the first half of the decade – went abroad at the impressionable age, it was with rifles in their hands rather than manuscript paper. The Second World War deprived them of educational adventures, though, revealingly, a 1929 boy, Kenneth Leighton, also made it to Italy to study with Petrassi, and this might be why Leighton, while always recognisable to the listener, is curiously unplaceable in connection with which of his British contemporaries influenced him.

Each generation of British composers is awash with names, most of whom, naturally, will fall into neglect and oblivion, or might never rise above anonymity. But each generation also has at least one or two well-known established figures that give a shape and identity to their time. Who were the headline acts in the 1920s generation? And here again, the mind might go blank. In desperation I turned to *Fairest Isle*, a book published by the BBC in 1995 to accompany a year-long celebration of British music.[2] At the back is a six-page 'Chronology of 500 British Composers', starting with Saint Godric (c.1069–1170)

---

2 David Fraser (ed.), *Fairest Isle: BBC Radio 3 Book of British Music* (BBC Books, 1995).

and ending with Thomas Adès, then only 24 years old. The 1920–29 list is a litany of half-remembered names, often recalled for the wrong reason. Here is Peter Racine Fricker (b.1920), immortalised not for his music but as a joke in Kingsley Amis's novel *Lucky Jim* ('Aren't you going to stay for the P Racine Fricker?'). Here is Geoffrey Bush (b.1920) – no, not the communist chap, that was *Alan* born 20 years earlier. Here is Arthur Butterworth (b.1923) – no, it was *George* who set *A Shropshire Lad*. Then come Iain Hamilton (1922), Anthony Milner (1925), John Buller (1927) and Wilfred Josephs (1927). Josephs, like Leighton, made it abroad, studying with Max Deutsch in Paris, having originally trained as a dentist before deciding on a lifetime of counterpoint rather than cavities. He wrote the theme tune for the BBC's serial *I, Claudius* (1976), but how many people know this? My immediate thought reading the list was that these are the sorts of names that, when mentioned, get a reply along the lines of, 'Yes, I *think* I once heard a rather well-made wind quintet by him.' Gratefully I stumble on Alun Hoddinott (1929), who is now a concert hall in Cardiff.

An earlier review of English music as revealing as *Fairest Isle* is Hugh Wood's chapter in *European Music in the Twentieth Century* (1961).[3] It is a period piece, and one from which the author somewhat distanced himself in later years. But it shows that in 1961, the 1920s generation was already being forced to the edge of the argument. While sandwiched between the Walton-Bush-Tippett generation and the emerging 1930s composers, we find, revealingly, that it is the figure of Benjamin Britten (b.1913), standing at the apex of Wood's list of composers ('He stands alone, and is our best claim to a composer of

---

3 Hugh Wood, 'English Contemporary Music', *European Music in the Twentieth Century*, ed., Howard Hartog (Pelican Books, 1957, revised ed., 1961), pp. 145–70.

world rank') that might be part of the problem. Britten eclipsed the 1920s boys by being too close in age. His major works first achieving worldwide prominence and sweeping all before them were in the years 1945–55, the same years when the 1920s boys would have been reaching maturity and establishing themselves. The 1930s generation was far enough away in age to treat Britten as a father figure, and thereby absorb what they wanted from him, while also voicing the necessary rejections and renunciations that each generation feels for those that preceded them. But the 1920s boys were lumbered with Britten in a position akin to a dazzling older brother.

Today's musicological discourse is rejecting of concepts of genius, finding it a quality ripe to dismantle and mock. Fair enough. But harder to eradicate is the effect genius has on those around it. Think how hard it must be to sit down to compose an opera when a composer a few miles away can knock out something of the quality of *Albert Herring* in four months, and do so using musical materials that are both simple and direct but also fresh. Indeed, Britten posed a particular problem for the half-generation that followed him, the 1920s boys. He demonstrated how a musical idiom that was essentially traditional could be revitalised. But such an extraordinary achievement needed time to feed into the soil, to embed itself and thus to be available to other composers in a way that avoided direct plagiarism. Britten, genius or not, had an effect. His work resonated; it impinged.

Today, the name that does jump out from the list of 1920s boys as still a presence in our current musical consciousness is Malcolm Arnold (b.1921). The film music ensured Arnold's reach was always stretched beyond the concert-going public. And the orchestral dances and light music remain a staple of the amateur orchestral repertoire. But Arnold never fitted, even when alive, into any obvious place in the British music scene, and his personal issues have sadly disguised the true achievement of his radical music. Arnold's symphonies are now gaining acceptance: they are an extended cycle of nine works, and since neither Britten nor Walton produced a cycle (and Tippett's four symphonies are also so different to each other as to make talk of a cycle too problematic) there is potential space for an Arnold cycle.

As a genre, symphonies are one way of getting a handle on many of the 1920s boys. They were at the heart of Robert Simpson's (b.1921) output. If a crude shorthand has Arnold as the Mahlerian symphonist, pulling in popular idioms and a diversity of material in his symphonies, then Simpson can be taken as the balancing 'Sibelius/Nielsen' northern symphonist. His magisterial cycles of symphonies and string quartets are typified by an almost polemical agenda to reject Germanic European modernism with the radicalism of Scandinavia. Yet more characteristic of this branch of British music is that mocking description 'Cheltenham Symphony', defined by Peter Pirie as works that were 'in simple-minded sonata form, simple-minded tonality, and simple-minded faith in a scissors-and-paste method of composition'.[4] For David Drew they were simply 'ersatz', in which 'the orchestral garb is dungarees at best and old sacking at worst.'[5]

By the 1990s the critical perspective had changed only slightly – allowing a touch of irony into the mix. We could admit to a sneaking, guilty, patronising delight in these works as long as they were taken only as period pieces, not living works of art. These symphonies sat in the corner like odd bits of

4 Peter Pirie, *The English Musical Renaissance* (Victor Gollancz, 1979).
5 David Drew, 'The Cheltenham Symphony', *The New Statesman*, 20th July 1962, p. 92.

clunky furniture; lacking style, they accrued their slither of
value only by being defined by that catch-all umbrella term,
'vintage'. Stephen Johnson gets this attitude spot on: 'To many
today the label brings unavoidable associations with an
orchestral sound redolent of London fogs, austerity menus and
the creaky film acting and *mise en scène* so wickedly lampooned
by Harry Enfield.'[6] The Cheltenham symphonists are not
exclusively 1920s boys – one thinks of Edmund Rubbra (b.1901)
most obviously – but enough names are: Racine Fricker, Arnold,
John Veale (b.1922), Hamilton and Bush (Geoffrey!).

Fast-forward to now, and the time is still out of joint for the
1920s boys. Even in their centenary years they have been fated
to remain obscured. The worldwide Covid pandemic dealt a
blow to Arnold and Simpson's celebrations in 2021. And the
critical mood also demanded, rightly, that the 1920s girls, overlooked and patronised in their day, should now finally be valued
and appreciated. Hundredth birthday concert slots and recording projects were thus filled with Ruth Gipps (b.1921) and
Doreen Carwithen (b.1922). One obvious name omitted so far
has been of a 1920s girl thankfully still with us – and one of the
finest voices of them all: Thea Musgrave (b.1928). Resident in
the USA for many years, Musgrave has been somewhat
neglected in British concert halls. But her 90th birthday was
marked properly with the award of the Queen's Medal for
Music in 2017. Though, as always in Britain, these awards can
feel as if given for longevity rather than anything else. As Alan
Bennett put it, 'If you can eat a boiled egg at 90 in England they
think you deserve a Nobel Prize.'

---

6 David Fraser (ed.), *Fairest Isle: BBC Radio 3 Book of British Music* (BBC Books,
1995), p. 100.

Is it even worth using the centenaries to raise a flag, when the 1930s generation are dying out now – Maxwell Davies, Birtwistle, Bennett, Maw, Payne, Wood all no longer there?

I think so. Centenaries can be like royal jubilees – a way of marking time – but also a way of trying to get an angle on a slice of the past. Indeed, if the championing of Gipps and Carwithen in their centenary years means that in future no writer will be allowed to publish unchallenged an essay referring to 'the 1920s boys', then at least something has been challenged and changed. At worst the 1920s composers will be left in years to come in a no-person's land, rather than a no-man's land.

∞

Such a *tour d'horizon* might seem excessively negative to introduce the 1920s boy that is the focus of this centenary study, Stephen Dodgson. But without context it would be impossible to answer the simple question, 'How has Dodgson's music fared so far?'

In some ways he was not typical of the 1920s boys even at the time, and so escapes some of the negative images we have of his generation. There is, for example, no body of mature symphonies (though an early symphony in E flat composed in 1953 won a Royal Philharmonic Society prize). Nor was there any film music. He established other facets to his career, working extensively as both teacher and radio broadcaster. But such activities often prove, and have done so in Dodgson's case, ephemeral in the mind of the wider public.

In other respects, however, Dodgson's work is holding up better than most of his contemporaries. One reason is practical: his estate is well organised and has been active in supporting performances and recordings, and now the production of this centenary volume. Money exists and has been wisely spent. And the result is that the music lover can now easily access most of Dodgson's work from the full-length opera *Margaret Catchpole* to the complete cycle of string quartets and many smaller instrumental works.

Another factor helping Dodgson's ongoing profile is that he has become known for his rich body of music for guitar, from concertos to ensemble works and individual compositions. Though not a player of the instrument himself, Dodgson's output is marked by his extraordinary understanding of the qualities of the guitar, and he was wise to contribute with genuine sympathy and creativity to a medium where he was less likely to be pushed aside by established names from previous centuries.

Listeners coming to Stephen Dodgson's music for the first time could not do better than starting with the Concerto No. 1 for guitar and chamber orchestra (1956). In this work one hears immediately so many of the fingerprints of his well-crafted and enjoyable musical idiom. The thematic material which opens the concerto is simple (essentially an arpeggiated idea with a scale motif that follows). But, as with Britten, Dodgson can make something so basic also fresh and characterful. Throughout the concerto one notices an economy and clarity of orchestral texture, including wonderful unison passages in the wind, reminiscent of a certain French idiom filtered through a British composer like Lennox Berkeley. Dodgson himself commented:

I've always believed that the exact placing and timing of the orchestral tutti is the paramount consideration in any concerto's design. With the guitar, it is, of course, vital to avoid confusion in anyone's mind about when the soloist should be heard and, conversely, where the orchestra may be given its head. I have tried to make a virtue of this necessity. The slow movement, for example, depends for its architecture on the span and precise point of arrival of its single passage for the whole orchestra.[7]

That central slow movement also captures a great sense of emotional depth, particularly in its closing passage that cadences onto the note E. The finale, while not boisterous and extravagant in the extreme manner of Malcolm Arnold, does share something of Arnold's lightness of touch and spot-on sense of pacing.

Naturally comparisons come into the mind of a listener exploring any composer's music for the first time. Francis Routh found that for Dodgson, 'Those composers with whom he has a particular affinity are Debussy, Shostakovich, Janáček, in whose work he admires power, subtlety, and economy.'[8] One can hear the logic of such a statement in many works, but the more one gets to know Dodgson's music the more the individual character of his musical voice becomes recognisable.

A strong sense of place is often present in the music. Most obviously two of his stage works, the four-act *Margaret Catchpole* (1979) and the earlier, smaller-scale 'narrative entertainment' *Cadilly* (1969), are set in East Anglia. Obvious comparisons with Britten can be quickly acknowledged, but any debt is repaid with interest. The opening bars of *Cadilly* are a masterclass in how a composer can immediately conjure a sense of landscape, of reedy banks, the flow of the river and the sense of expansive sky. The reader of the score is amazed that such precise sense of location and mood can arise from such seemingly simple musical materials. But then, as Routh noted, 'The underlying

7 Francis Routh, *Contemporary British Music* (Macdonald, 1972).
8 ibid.

elements of tonal music – rhythm, harmony, melody – are in his case uncomplicated in essence, though capable of considerable complexity in detail.'

Stephen Dodgson's orchestral music has so far yet to gain the recognition it deserves. He focused much of his attention from the 1980s onwards on a series of single-movement scores entitled 'Essays'. Music lovers are fortunate to have an album recorded of the first five essays in performances by the Royal Scottish National Orchestra conducted by David Lloyd-Jones. Unlike the symphony, which Hans Keller defined as the 'large-scale integration of contrasts', in Dodgson's orchestral essays, he prefers 'to treat the orchestra boldly, as an integrated body and with ideas concentrated and unified more than contrasted'.[9] The important point to grasp is that Dodgson's essays are less built on the drama of confrontation and a narrative of finding connections and resolution, and more on exploring a musical idea intensely from the premise that it is already integrated and whole. What this means in terms of rhetoric is that the music has a different kind of energy and harmonic propulsion.

For example, *Essay No. 2* (1981) is a vigorous scherzo that focuses on and explores obsessively a short number of triple-time rhythmic ideas. Orchestration and texture (there are ingenious uses of orchestral piano and xylophone) are as much part of the music's means of communication as pitch. But any fear for the first-time listener that we will experience a strictly cerebral music – Dodgson as essay-writer of a philosophical tract, for example – is quickly dispersed by the wonderful warmth of much of the harmony: not too far from the sunlit Mediterranean soundscape of post-war Walton. In contrast,

---

9 John Warrack, liner notes to *Essay Nos. 1–5*, Royal Scottish National Orchestra / David Lloyd-Jones, Dutton Epoch CDLX 7236 (2010).

Essay No. 5 (1985), a dramatic allegro, appears to be taking a step closer to the symphonic argument of drama and conflict. But the closing section of this work brilliantly undercuts any sense of unquestioning resolution when a snare drum interrupts the sense of approach to the final cadence. And Dodgson pulls off one of the most coveted compositional effects at the end: to finish a few bars before the listener expects it!

For a composer who read so widely and with a deep love of poetry, it is no surprise that Dodgson made such an extensive and accomplished contribution to the genre of song. The three new discs of his songs, issued by SOMM Recordings, are a superb introduction to the variety and skill of his output in this area. Taking the first disc as an example, two very different settings show his extraordinary ability to capture in simple and direct musical motifs the essence of a setting, while allowing space for surprises and a sense of play. Take the setting for voice and guitar of 'Trotty Wagtail' from the *Four Poems of John Clare* (1961) written for Wilfred Brown. Dodgson achieves here a lightness of touch that never becomes derivative and the use of gentle syncopation in the vocal lines ensures the music has a delightfully unsteady waddle. Capturing a completely different emotional world is the setting of 'Psyche' that opens the cycle *Tideways* (1950). If forced to save only one work of Dodgson's, this is the one I would choose. The piano accompaniment's gentle arpeggios are monotonous and yet simultaneously poised with potentiality as well as a latent eroticism. The vocal line is powerfully focused by being restricted to essentially stepwise movement and the resulting flow of semitonal movement caresses the ear, hovering, 'as air that brusheth by one / Close'. There is a telling shift harmonically at the line, 'And music flowing through me seemed to open / Mine eyes upon new colours' that seems to promise a wholly new expansion tonally, but is quickly denied as the opening bars reassert themselves. The effect is powerful, creating the sense of claustrophobia and trance.

What this celebratory volume aims to do is to foreground the music of Stephen Dodgson, allowing a spotlight to linger on this particular part of the British musical landscape so that listeners and performers can engage with the music in the way the composer wished: with enjoyment and pleasure. The book aims to capture his voice, both musically and in terms of his thoughts, by providing a sequence of his own writings in which he discussed his working methods, music that inspired him, and ideas that fascinated (or sometimes even repelled) him. Then, after a series of short tributes from friends and colleagues, there follows a sequence of essays exploring various parts of his output by a group of specially assembled experts. This is the first sustained critical engagement with his music, and long overdue. What the editors of this volume hope is that it will help maintain interest in his compositions and begin the process of further critical engagement.

This 1920s boy is to have his centenary moment.

Dancing to the Music of his Time
Stephen Dodgson: A Biographical Note

THOMAS HYDE with JANE CLARK DODGSON

'A shilling life will give you all the facts', WH Auden famously wrote, sceptical of the easy reading of the relationship between the life and the work of any creative artist. Do biographical facts get you closer to understanding the work or do they just get in the way? One can never know whether, given an alternative house, partner and job, an artist would have produced the same, similar or different work. It is true that time and place can be more of a general guide. On meeting a composer's music for the first time one can often locate its date to at least a particular century, and often decide whether it be French, German, British or not. But anything more particular and the links of biography and work become more suspect. As with all composers, Stephen Dodgson's life and work are linked: this life produced this work. But the life cannot explain why the work is as it is.

If biography can tell us the where and when of a work's creation, why it was commissioned and by whom, nevertheless what happens in the imaginative act of *doing the work* remains mysterious. The director of films and documentaries about a composer faces a particular challenge: writing music simply isn't dramatic. The camera hovers at the figure seated at the desk or at the piano writing. But how long can such an image hold the attention? And anyway, what exactly *is* being shown? At the opening of Tony Palmer's film of William Walton, the elderly composer sits at his piano showing off his pencils and erasers ('I spend my life rubbing out what I have written'). Eventually he looks into the camera and, with a mixture of alarm and resignation, says, 'What are you going to do? *Look* at me?'

In reality, what tends to happen is that the director cuts away from the figure scribbling at the desk and opts for more exciting dramatic images of landscapes or city scenes, leading to a facile implication that such images are *explaining* what the music is about. This impulse is understandable but was ripe for mockery, and reviewing a television programme about the Italian composer Luigi Nono, Clive James mocked the technique:

> There was also footage of his fellow Venetians performing alien-ated tasks, such as selling fish to one another. The implication was that it would need Nono's music to give such tasks meaning. It was painfully evident that Nono lacks the mental equipment to take in the suggestion that his job is not to make selling fish as interesting as his music, but to make his music as interesting as selling fish.[1]

(Luigi Nono might have been musical worlds away from Stephen Dodgson, but we will meet him briefly once more in this chapter.)

The truth is that composers, more often than not, live simple lives designed on gaining themselves enough free time for the extended periods of concentration required for creative work. Other activities, be it performing, teaching or managing their bank accounts, are fitted around the central activity that remains

1 Clive James, *The Crystal Bucket* (Jonathan Cape Ltd, 1981), p. 133.

a vocation. In later life, Dodgson got to know *The Sunday Times* executive Ron Hall and his first wife, Ruth, a talented pianist. An idea was mooted for an interview, but the feature was eventually abandoned when Ruth, in horror, announced to the composer, 'I just can't do this: you are just too boring!'

What then is this biographical note, placed near the start of this centenary volume, attempting to do? Certainly, it aims to place Dodgson's life in context: to set out where and when he worked on his music. And this context, that of a comfortable upper middle-class background, helps to explain the shape of Dodgson's career. Auden complained that English cultural life 'was a family life', and indeed bonds of family, school, forces and profession often dictated how and what kinds of commissions came the composer's way. There is a recognisably rhythmic quality to Dodgson's life and in this respect he can sometimes appear akin to Nicholas Jenkins, the figure at the centre of Anthony Powell's novel sequence, *A Dance to the Music of Time*, but moving around a generation later: his web extends from his home in Barnes through music college and into the BBC; friendships are formed, and requests for music naturally arrive. In obvious and delightful ways, those whom he knew and when he knew them explain why he wrote the pieces he did when he did, 'hand in hand in intricate measure: stepping slowly, methodically, sometimes a trifle awkwardly, in evolutions that take recognisable shape; or breaking into seemingly meaningless gyration, while partners disappear only to reappear again, once more giving pattern to the spectacle'.[2]

---

2 Anthony Powell, *A Question of Upbringing* (William Heinemann Ltd, 1951), pp. 1–2.

So, let us allow Dodgson the composer to become Stephen the man.

∞

Stephen Cuthbert Vivian Dodgson was born on 17th March 1924 in Chelsea, London, into a distinguished and artistic upper middle-class family. His father, John Arthur Dodgson (1890–1969), was a symbolist artist born at Murree, Bengal, India, to an Indian Army officer and his aristocratic wife. The Dodgson family also included Campbell Dodgson (1867–1948), the art historian and museum curator who was the Keeper of Prints and Drawings at the British Museum, and further along the branch of cousins in the distance was Charles Lutwidge Dodgson, more famously known as the author Lewis Carroll. John briefly studied at Oxford but soon left to attend the Slade School of Fine Art in 1913. It was here that he met Stephen's mother, 'Margaret Valentine Pease (1889–1952) – known to all as 'Val', a young woman from a Northumbrian family of small bankers. Though his father later taught at both the Chelsea and Camberwell schools of art, he had private means, though much of it had gone by the time it reached his son. Rather, it was from his mother's side of the family that their composer son inherited his financial acumen and canniness, always able to invest wisely and make money work for him. John and Margaret were married in April 1916. Stephen was their third and youngest child, and their only son.

Though Stephen was to live at his family's home until the age of 33 when he moved to Barnes, this disguises several points of upheaval and change. He was educated at Berkhamsted School, Hertfordshire, before attending Stowe School, Buckinghamshire. He loved his years at Stowe and particularly enjoyed learning Russian. But in 1942, at the age of 18 he was, as expected, called up and he joined the Royal Navy. Initially posted to Sri Lanka (then Ceylon) he went on to be part of anti-submarine warfare, escorting convoys in the Battle of the Atlantic. This was dangerous, with many ships being sunk, but he recalled his relief when the Armistice was declared, and he witnessed German submarines coming up from under the ship he was on. But like many who had seen active service, Stephen was never eager to talk about it.

After the Navy, Stephen decided music was to be the core of his life. He had private composition lessons with Bernard Stevens before he went to the Royal College of Music, London, in 1946. His principal study was horn, but composition was his real passion. His studies with RO Morris were to instil a love of early music, notably by Thomas Morley and William Byrd, while lessons with Patrick Hadley and Antony Hopkins were more focused on the practicalities of learning the craft of contemporary composition. As befits many young composers, he began his professional career by making his mark in competitions. In 1948 he won the Cobbett Memorial Prize for a Fantasy Quartet (for string quartet), and two RPS prizes followed, for the Variations for Orchestra (1949) and the Symphony in E flat (1953). Meanwhile, in 1949 he won an RCM Octavia Scholarship, which encouraged students to spend time abroad, previous recipients including Grace Williams, who went to Egon Wellesz in Vienna, and Elizabeth Maconchy, who went to Karel Jirák in Prague. Famously, Benjamin Britten, another Octavia scholar, was to be discouraged from his hopes to study with Alban Berg. Rather than opting for formal study, Stephen chose Rome, living in the British School in the city for six months and indulging his passion for Roman ruins and ancient architecture. He then went travelling, and it is at this juncture we briefly meet Luigi Nono, who found Stephen not only a flat in Venice but also a doctor when he suffered food poisoning.

Returning to Britain in the spring of 1950, Stephen settled into his career of balancing commissions and teaching. Initially he taught at The Farmhouse School in Buckinghamshire while continuing to live at home. Much as Peter Maxwell Davies was to do a decade later at Cirencester Grammar School, Stephen composed operas and instrumental pieces for the pupils, finding a fruitful balance between producing music that was of immediate use and the new demands made on his compositional technique. Economy of means and precision of texture and timbre were always to be characteristic of his music, and his experience in schools helped to crystalise this facet of his work. Alongside, he was increasingly supported and promoted by leading professional musicians, including oboist Evelyn Barbirolli, harpist Maria Korchinska and the violinist Neville Marriner. He was even programmed by Gerald Finzi and the Newbury String Players, though it is claimed that Finzi found his style 'rather ungrateful'[3].

Stephen's mother died in 1952 and this unbalanced his relationship with his father, who had always been an overbearing and dominant influence on his son, notably in his views and taste in art. His father remarried, and when his stepmother persuaded John to move to Suffolk, Stephen finally moved out to Barnes where he was to put down his roots.

---

3 The work in question is Dodgson's *Divertimento* for flute and strings (1950). Writing to Robin Milford on 22nd May 1951, Finzi described the work as, 'interesting but rather ungrateful writing, which noone except the composer, a nice chap, enjoyed!'. Dodgson himself later rejected the score and it was unpublished (see *Gerald Finzi's Letters 1915–1956*, ed. Diana McVeagh, The Boydell Press, 2021, pp. 748, 757).

Essential to this process of putting down new roots was meeting the harpsichordist Jane Clark at Christmas 1958 when visiting his family in Suffolk. He had already taken an interest in the instrument and composed for it as a result of his friendship with the Czech musicologist and player Stanislav Heller. But there is no doubt that Jane further encouraged and inspired his love for early and Baroque music. From Suffolk, Jane was working in London having studied at the Guildhall and then in Paris with the Belgian keyboardist Aimée van de Wiele. Though she 'didn't know much modern music, except *Peter Grimes* – the Suffolk link!', she met up with him again in London and was taken to a BBC recording of one of his works. A page-turner was needed for the harpist, and Jane was co-opted into the role. A curious first date. They were engaged three months later, despite his sharp elbows discovered when playing piano duets together, and married in 1959.

Shortly before he met Jane two essential strands to Stephen's working life became focused. Firstly, he was back at the Royal College of Music, having started to teach at the Junior RCM in 1956. The association was to continue for the rest of his working life. In 1965 he became Professor of Composition and Music Theory at the RCM, holding this post, which normally could be fitted into three days a week, until he retired in 1982. Secondly, since 1957 he had become a regular broadcaster for BBC radio. Not only was there incidental music, a result of his friendship with the producer Raymond Raikes, but Stephen also became a well-loved voice as a presenter of review shows and documentaries on music. Producer John Lade, who lived in Chelsea, was the contact. Having founded *Record Review*, Lade immediately asked Stephen to contribute. Appearances on *Music Magazine* followed. As happened later with Michael Berkeley, music lovers came to feel they knew him personally from his friendly

presence on the radio waves. His broadcasting work and incidental music compositions were admired as well as lucrative.
He composed very little film music. One attempt he took to
Glasgow to be recorded by Muir Mathieson, who threw it on the
floor saying, 'no bloody timings!'.

Stephen's life settled into a successful middle age of professional
fulfilment, his timetable dictated by the shape of the academic
year. Augusts, when free of teaching, were strictly protected
time for composition. Holidays with Jane tended to be around
Easter and in June. Though even when at home in Barnes, he
found it easy to switch off from creative work once out of the
house. Bike rides became a passion. Later, following retirement
from the RCM, he found a new second home at Jane's mother's
house in Suffolk, not far from the Fens. With an upright piano
put in, he enjoyed combining composing with winter walks.
The short opera *Cadilly* (1969) and other works were stirred by
the new environment. He willingly took up various committee
positions, including from 1986 as Chair of the National Youth
Wind Orchestra.

Among his passions were wine and bread-making. Jane
remembers extensive detours during holidays simply so he could
obtain a particular flour. He was a superb cook and an active
gardener. For his social life, he preferred theatre to concerts.

If we envisage that our imagined television documentary
maker might take fright at all this calm, stable business-like
approach to composing and teaching, then we could instead
return to the image of Stephen at the centre of his own web of
friends and colleagues all engaged in their professional dance.
For his creativity sprang from the continual need of the people
around him; whether a work for an unusual combination of
instruments or a new overture for Gilbert and Sullivan's *The*

Mikado (this was almost written over the phone and still brings in royalties).

For example, the path that led to him becoming well known for his music for guitar. He had originally composed for the instrument in the 1950s when a Russian actor Alexis Chesnakov asked for some folksong settings. Friendship with Julian Bream resulted in the *Prelude, Nocturne and Toccata* (1952), though Bream strained his arm which delayed the premiere. The Guitar Concerto No. 1 similarly was due for premiere by Bream, but problems with dates led to the first soloist being a 17-year-old John Williams who also became a life-long collaborator and went to commission the second guitar concerto. Later, from 1997, he struck up a close working relationship with the recorder player John Turner, which added to his output for the instrument. This stretched back to works for his one-time student Richard Harvey and even earlier incidental music for a 1970 BBC radio production of *Perkin Warbeck* which featured David Munrow. And closest of all, perhaps, was trumpeter Philip Jones. As well as original works for the Philip Jones Brass Ensemble the friendship produced a series of arrangements by Stephen. This started on holiday in the Alps when Philip complained that there was not enough repertoire for the ensemble. Jane suggested arrangements of Scarlatti – feeling that 'Stephen understood the potential of it – since some of the sonatas were based on Spanish band music'.

Of composing friends, Stephen was close to Joseph Horowitz who taught alongside him at the Royal College of Music. Kenneth Leighton was also a long-standing friend ever since they travelled to the USSR together in 1960 (Stephen learnt Russian from the music critic Martin Cooper while at school in Stowe). Another close colleague was John Gardner, famous now for his carol *Tomorrow Shall be my Dancing Day*. Gardner,

director of music at St Paul's Girls School, commissioned
Stephen to write a cantata. On his first visit to the school,
Gardner grabbed him by the scruff of his neck and marched him
down a corridor to the lavatory. He flung the door open and
pointed saying, 'To think Gustav Holst shat there!'

And what of the musical figures at a distance, unmet but
dancing in his imagination? His interest in early and Baroque
music has already been touched on. He felt less inclined to the
late Romantics, preferring Johann Strauss to Richard. He felt
far from Mahler and the Second Viennese School. With this in
mind it is not surprising that while he revered Benjamin Britten
he was less keen on a work like *Death in Venice*. He preferred
early Tippett to the later music, which he felt had got badly
clogged up. Janáček was possibly his most passionate influence. But Russian music, notably Shostakovich and Prokofiev,
was also a favourite. Verdi was preferred to Puccini. All this
fed into the creation of Stephen's own musical idiom, which
Guy Rickards outlined as 'written mostly in an agreeable if
occasionally challenging modern tonal idiom, cosmopolitan
rather than overtly British in style, influenced by early and
Baroque music and Janáček as much as English pastoralism ...
His mature style was one of refinement, sitting somewhere
between Post-Romanticism and Neo-Classicism, but individual works often had quirky, even spectral sides to them.'[4]

As writers in this volume note, however, Stephen's idiom
always manages to escape classification. This would surely have
pleased him. As early as 1960, in a profile of young composers
published in *The Musical Times*, Stephen was defined as belong-
ing to no school, and regarding such schools 'as refuges for

---

4 Guy Rickards, 'Obituaries: Stephen Dodgson', *Gramophone*, Vol. 91 (June
2013), p. 25.

unadventurous minds. He believes the ideas contained in a piece of music to be far more important than the language in which they are expressed.'[5]

Stephen's last years were blighted by dementia, with a trumpet concerto his last completed work in 2011. He died in London on 13th April 2013 at the age of 89.

---

5 'The Younger Generation', *The Musical Times*, Vol. 101 No. 1405 (March 1960), p. 148.

PART 1

The Composer's Voice

When we think of 'the composer's voice' we might immediately consider the sounds and personality that emerge from the music itself. But with Stephen Dodgson we have a case of a composer whose actual voice, the lilt and charm of his spoken accent, was known to millions of music lovers through his activities as a national radio broadcaster.

This selection from Dodgson's extensive archive of scripts and articles aims to capture the character of the man himself in his professional life as a composer. The opening essay is the most extended description he provided of how he went about writing music. The essays that follow reflect on particular works and collaborations.

1. Personal View of a Composer

(OCTOBER 1991)

I suppose it's only natural people should be curious how a composer goes about his task. How *do* you get your ideas? Where do they *come* from? When I meet strangers, those are the most usual sort of questions, and needless to say they're just about impossible to answer. If the enquirer doesn't lose interest trying to make head or tail of my efforts to be coherent about something I've never understood myself, then perhaps we move on to rather easier questions like: What are you working on right now? How long do you work each day?

As to that second one, my mind goes back to a book of interviews with British composers published about 25 years ago, in which, to start with, each was asked a few basic questions, including how much time they spent composing each day. One or two, it seemed, hardly had time to do anything else. But Malcolm Arnold replied, 'as little as possible', which had a greater ring of truth than all the rest, and which also neatly avoided saying how long it actually was. In fact, I think it's a question composers can be oddly shy about; and I'm not proposing to be frightfully candid about it myself.

There's certainly one popular conception about composing what (for lack of a better term) is called 'serious music', and that is that it's a time-consuming and laborious business. 'You mean you compose for choirs and orchestras?' an incredulous voice will say; 'Such an array of different performers – the drums, the violins, the sopranos, the basses – doesn't it take months just to write it all down?'

Maybe so. But that part, you explain, anyone can do with sufficient tenacity, some experience, and a reasonable training behind them. '*That* part of it isn't so unlike office work,' I'll say, warming to the subject, 'rather like an architect.' Your musical score has a similar function to his plans and elevations. He has to be intelligible to the contractors. The eventual building will hopefully stand up, be practical, and the client may even perhaps like it.

In these electronic days, there are ways of composing music which offer tempting shortcuts; and the pop-music industry specially has become heavily dependent upon them. The methods we assume Chopin and Liszt to have employed – their compositions starting life as improvisations – could be made miles easier today. Though I have to say my imagination doesn't quite stretch to glimpsing Chopin, clad in headphones, elaborating his intricate pianism at an electronic keyboard linked to a computer system. And I might as well confess right away that I actually rather *enjoy* the old, longhand methods, and still prefer writing music with a proper pen with a proper nib in it.

And that's probably not the only way I'm a bit out of date. For instance, I'm old-fashioned enough to find the office-work aspect of composition positively beneficial just because it does take time, does require patience, but mainly because the slow pace focuses my attention on detail. My excitement in music – other people's just as much as my own – is never sufficiently sustained by the effect, the emotion, the colour or the atmosphere alone. I'm not satisfied unless the meaning of all the contributing strands is eloquent. Which is much the same thing as saying that craftsmanship is essential to any work of art. Except that I would add that craftsmanship itself can be inspired.

Inspiration! If it wasn't for inspiration what excuse would we composers have for not working an eight-hour day like other responsible citizens? Our claim to being capable of inspiration allows us 'not to feel like it today', to mooch round the house unable to settle to anything else, and being domestically a thorough nuisance.

Was it Arthur Sullivan who said composing was nine-tenths hard work? And without that willing investment, the muse's ten per cent could never be vouchsafed. In these liberated days when we all expect our share of things as of right, that may sound a bit of a relic of the Victorian work ethic, but I've never known a successful composer who dared dispute it.

In so far as I've any confidence of experiencing even ten seconds of inspiration, I'm convinced that keeping steadily at work on one's craft is the only hope that I may. Just occasionally, a whole morning's work will pass in a flash, and I'll have three pages of scribbles, not even on proper manuscript paper. Yet there, as I break off, I'm aware of being in possession of all the raw material I need for a substantial piece. It's amazing how slender such a sketch can be, yet complete in essence.

Come the afternoon and the weather's fine, and no boring claims on my time, I'll leap on a bicycle. I may do something useful like visiting the local market – which is fun. Or take a spin round Richmond Park, which is also fun, but at the age of 67 seems to take a bit more effort than it used to. Back home over a cup of tea, I'll decide the activities for the rest of the day. I've grown cannier than I was. Hitherto I'd have dashed in, expecting instantly to fix that inspiring morning work in indisputably correct notation. Now, some managing-like gnome tends to intervene. 'Not now,' he nudges, 'better correct those proofs which have been lying about untended all week. Save your creative effort for tomorrow when you're fresh.' I normally yield to this gnome. He seems to talk sense.

I've never been one for the midnight oil. On those occasions when I've burnt it, I've seldom liked the result next day. And there's a chain reaction which I also don't like; the sleepless night which follows, and the drained feeling which follows that, spoiling the next day's work. In the old days too, when I was more often tense and wakeful than I am now, I'd be struck with musical ideas in the middle of the night – vivid ones, the precise notes settling on the staves. I'd steal out of bed into my work room and scribble them down, for otherwise I knew they'd have vanished by daybreak. Shivering, I'd creep back to bed, cosy in the satisfaction of saving a brilliant spark from extinction. But the spark never once looked so brilliant when the full light of day shone on it, so now I yawn, turn over in bed and ignore the siren voices.

Although I often don't do things when I intend, I think I have to call myself an organised person. And this definitely includes my attitude to creative work. Just as all music must for me have vital rhythm, so must my way of working at it be rhythmic. If I can bring myself to work really intensively throughout the morning, my instinct is to leave work of that degree of intensity till another equally organised session the next day. Each session has a beginning and an end, and a rhythm to sustain it. And I plan them to be like that in advance. It's the equivalent of a rehearsal, and I actually like to think of it that way because it sharpens the reality of musical performance with every note I write. And when I finish the session, I pack all my loose pages away in a cupboard out of sight, and I'm strict with myself not getting them out till my next working session comes around. My object is to put it out of my mind, to distance myself from it, hoping to gain an observer's view of what I've done. Sometimes it's best to be *super* strong-minded and lock sketches away for a week or two so as to enlarge the distance between you and it still more. Prokofiev is reported to have had the habit of working at a number of different projects simultaneously, and I've always supposed this was his reason. Also there's the thought that if one piece gets stuck, one of the others may be persuaded to move.

I work in a ground-floor room overlooking a quiet street. Most of the passers-by are on foot. I watch and am watched. If I see an acquaintance, we smile and wave. So, obviously I'm not of the Ivory Tower school. I don't at all hanker for a room apart, cossetted in silence. I know I'd find it oppressive and unnatural. If I feel distracted, working in full view so to speak, then that's a good barometer that my concentration's below par, and that in turn is a sure sign that my efforts at the moment aren't convincing. But it's amazing how suddenly they take a turn for the better. Equally astonishing is the lightning speed with which impulse and imagination can vanish. I've never found out if my experience is unusual or the norm, but at least I've learnt to take it philosophically; and it's only when entire days go by that I begin to hate the whole frustrating business and conclude that if I ever had a talent it's certainly deserted me now. I comfort myself remembering that Dvořák used to think that *each* piece he completed was his last; that his gift would any day just leave him as inexplicably as it had come.

Another indication that I've no place in an Ivory Tower is the telephone in my room, and moreover I answer it. There's only one sort of call I can't stand. It begins, 'Are you working?' 'Yes,' I say, waiting for more. 'Well I'll only keep you a moment,' and then follows a long story, ending very likely with my agreeing to make another phone call or two; or perhaps it's an urgent request for a testimonial. 'I took the liberty of giving your name; I hope you don't mind. They need to have something by Friday if you'd be so kind.'

This sort of thing really does test concentration and no mistake, and I'm sometimes surprised at my ability to shrug it off, and to find how readily I pick up the thread where I was forced to leave off. The funny thing is that I'd rather be interrupted and learn how to withstand it, than never be interrupted at all.

One reason for the telephone is of course that work arrives that way. I mean *paid* work. Another question I've grown accustomed to as a composer (and mostly delivered in very doubting tones), 'You mean it's your *profession*? You earn a *living* by it?'

'I never expected to,' I reply, 'but yes, amazingly, it is so and I do – well … more or less.' I explain how until recently I'd always taught music, how I still give courses from time to time, do occasional journalism and broadcasting, and work as an examiner. Nearly all of that has not only helped the budget but been enjoyable too, and in fact it's valuable in relating yourself to all the rest of music-making. It's so easy as a composer to drift into your own deceptive backwater rather than be buffeted about in the choppy waters out in the mainstreams.

So there once more I reveal myself as not being cut out for the Ivory Tower; I actually welcome being out there in the throng, kicked this way and that. You'll be misunderstood or thrust aside some of the time, but not always. The musical profession is intensely competitive; indeed it needs to be for its vitality. I much prefer to be given reminders of the fact, than to shut the door and hope they won't reach me. It's a bit like taking a cold bath every morning, though I certainly don't go to that extreme. And yes, I think I really would rather be snubbed than ignored.

Because of this, I have the reputation of being biddable. Someone finds themselves planning a festival programme involving a strange mixture of musicians, and no discoverable item anywhere in the repertoire to bring the whole lot together. That's the sort of moment when *my* name gets mentioned, and it may be on the other side of the world. A couple of years ago a fine organist-cum-harpsichordist I know phoned out of the blue from America. Would I accept a commission for a concerto for harpsichord with an ensemble of wind, brass and percussion? 'You must be joking,' I said. 'You'll never be heard!' The fact that he was himself to be the soloist made the proposal seem specially absurd – risking an impossibly difficult part from me, only to be swamped by a side-drum and a couple of trumpets. 'No, no!' he assured me. 'Of course we realise all that. It's the whole reason we turned to you. We decided if anyone could bring it off, you could.'

'It's a deal,' I said, flattered by his fine opinion. 'When do you want it?' And he named a date ridiculously near. With a second impossibility heaped on top of the first, the temptation became irresistible. 'I'd love to do it,' I said. 'Solving the impossible is always fun ...' ... And it was; including the invitation I later received to go to Texas and hear the result.

Source: Typed manuscript, dated 28th October 1991

∞

The resulting work for harpsichord, wind, brass and percussion referred to at the end of this essay is *Arlington Concertante* (1986). In a later article for the British Association of Symphonic Bands and Wind Ensembles' *Wind Magazine* (Summer 2003), Dodgson commented:

Arlington Concertante was a challenge indeed. This began with thematic character, which had to be 'friendly' to both camps; only the harpsichord allowed to make a speech, otherwise a conversation-piece but, importantly, able to build into a cohesive tutti sound now and then, thanks to the inbuilt staccato nature of the principal theme. Elsewhere, light percussion provided an intriguing link between the largely incompatible contestants. For me, it's a fascinating hybrid.

2. Piano Trios, Quartets and Quintets

(MARCH 1975)

Almost exactly 25 years ago, in March 1950 – the previous Anno Santo to the present one – I was travelling in a very slow train across the Apennines from Rome (where I'd been the fortunate holder of a scholarship) to Ancona. It was probably the kind of train that the Italians, with a fine sense of comedy, call an Accelerato. It was very very slow, and (perhaps for that reason) more or less empty. And what is I suppose quite a short journey was made to feel like crossing a continent.

I remember it as distinctly as I do, because, during it, I was struck with the strongest musical idea I'd so far experienced, and immediately decided that the medium it required was a piano quartet. Trying to scribble bits of it down filled in the time nicely. Some months later, back in England, the whole piece finally got itself composed; that strong idea mixed with a number of others, not all of which could be so described. A year or two later, it was one of my first compositions ever to be broadcast, and got my photograph into the *Radio Times* for the only time in my career. An exciting event, all in all, and the music still has the power to excite me now, though in parts rather, like the curate's egg.

What I don't recall was what so firmly decided me that my first glimpse of that musical idea on the Accelerato just had to be for piano quartet. To know it was a mixture of piano and strings is one thing. But how come I was so certain that there were three strings and not two or four? The strangely fascinating thing about this kind of decision is that they are made in a flash, are usually irreversible, and if there was an underlying reason you can't remember it even an hour later. In fact, I'd go so far as to say that if you can remember the reason, then the basic musical idea was probably not that strong and definite in character.

Anyway, that piano quartet of 25 years ago was the first of several works for piano and strings I've composed, and the only one that was solely my idea to write and not prompted by an invitation from specific players. In fact, if I hadn't been loaded with all sorts of other projects recently, I might easily during the past four years have written two more piano quartets, since two ensembles have independently asked me to write for them, and I entirely appreciate why they're choosy about reviving that old one.

The important point here is that piano quartets actually exist. I mean players form themselves into this ensemble on purpose to play its repertoire, starting from those two marvellous quartets – G minor and E flat – by Mozart, through Dvořák and Brahms to Chausson, Fauré, Copland and Martinů. But the contemporary end of the repertoire is thin, to say the least, and piano quartets are always on the look-out for interesting new material well-written for the medium. The only one that springs readily to my mind of the last few years is a characteristically bold composition by Kenneth Leighton.

With piano trios, the repertoire has a quite different character, but is possibly even more suggestive of forming an ensemble on purpose to play it. The medium is always absolutely true chamber music; and even that craggy, monolithic sort of writing that Shostakovich employs in his Piano Trio [No. 2] – one of his greatest chamber works I think – doesn't belong on the other side of that watershed, so difficult to pinpoint, which leads into the territory of concertante or quasi-symphonic music.

The piano trio is equally as short of modern repertoire as the piano quartet. And there's no doubt that the medium is very under-exploited in modern terms. And I don't mean experimental ideas, necessarily, but the many things suggested by Ravel, for instance, in his trio – one of the landmarks of the repertoire from earlier this century. There are many things in Ravel's trio which have never yet been followed up.

I can't help feeling that there's a certain prejudice among many composers for writing for the medium I'm considering. It must be that they're far more stimulated by combinations offering wider colour range and textural variety. And I suppose it's because I've appeared sympathetic to the medium for its own sake that I've twice been invited and have actually written piano trios.

And as to that prejudice which I think exists in many composers' minds; I remember Benjamin Frankel, perhaps a dozen years ago, saying very firmly that the combination – no matter what you did with it – was for him impossibly dated, inevitably associated in his estimation with café/pump-room styles, the chinking of tea cups and polite conversation. When I heard Benjamin Frankel say that, I thought I agreed with him; but I'm glad to say I managed to disagree later, and – with the greatest respect – I don't think either of the two piano trios I've written – whatever they do sound like – sound like that.

In this roundabout way, I at last arrive at the piano quintet. And the first thing to be said here is that piano quintets don't exist. Unlike the trios and quartets, there aren't ensembles formed specially for this repertoire. Yet there's no lack of opportunity to hear at least the four greatest works in the medium, all written within a period of under 50 years, stretching from Schumann in E flat in 1842 to Dvořák in A major in 1887. But the performances of those come about either when an existing string quartet specially asks a pianist to join them for the occasion, or through one of those open-ended ensembles, to whom no one instrumentation is any more central than any other. The variety which is so much demanded by modern times clearly needs this kind of ensemble. And, conversely, piano quintets as a collection just do not demand the formation of special ensembles to perform just them.

And there's another aspect too. Forgive me if you think it's too obvious for words, but it can easily be overlooked. Once you have a string quartet – in fact, imagine yourself a member of a good amateur string quartet. You get together to play. However beautiful their music, where's the temptation to get out the Schumann, Brahms, Franck or Dvořák quintets and import a loud unsubtle piano (to say nothing of the pianist) when you have the whole of the Haydn, Mozart and Beethoven quartet repertoire before you? This factor must in the Romantic age – which is indubitably the age of the piano quintet – have had its influence.

But there's also the factor of what a piano quintet sounds like, what you can do with it, what style suits it best, that has also had a limiting influence; not perhaps on how many piano quintets have been written, but how few really successful ones there seem to be. And this is where most of the rest of my random comments come in.

Forgetting Hummel for the moment – whose piano quintet must certainly be one of the first, let me start with the first real landmark, which is Schumann. Schumann's quintet is for me definitely the greatest of all his many chamber music works, and indeed one of the greatest things he ever wrote. Back to the wall, revolver to my head, I'd name it as the piano quintet I love most. It has such an exultant life about it, and so many superbly memorable ideas. There's a grandeur of manner about it too, which is not at all the Schumann of the piano miniatures and the songs. It's much more nearly the Schumann of the symphonies; those symphonies he's so often supposed to have overscored. But the piano quintet is beyond criticism in its scoring. It has a very definite feeling of orchestral tutti about it, with contrasting quieter passages, solo voices in dialogue over harmonic and rhythmic accompaniments. Another evident feature concerns the piano part, which is absolutely continuous. It has a bar or two's silence in the finale but is otherwise non-stop. Now this is not at all like a concerto, in which the solo part in the classical view was always constructed in large vaulting arches with the orchestral tuttis forming the main supportive piers of the edifice. Schumann's piano part is far more like the orchestral backbone; and in the strenuous sections the strings team up into unisons or strong chordal formations rather like pitting wind and brass as a body against the mass of the strings.

I used earlier the metaphor of the watershed dividing the territory of true chamber music from that of concertante and quasi-symphonic music. Schumann's quintet is emphatically on the farther side of that slope. And so in its own distinctive way is Brahms, opus 34 in F minor, written some 20 years later.

One of the interesting things here is that Brahms didn't know he was writing a piano quintet. It's a perpetually surprising thought to me that he wrote the whole piece as a string quintet first; performed it like that, not apparently a total success; particularly violinist and friend Joseph Joachim didn't think so. I take it that it was too tough, muscular and congested for the medium – too symphonic if you like.

Brahms then rewrote the work for two pianos, and in this form it won Clara Schumann's unqualified approval. However, Brahms was still not satisfied, and rewrote the work a third time – fantastic tenacity – arriving at last at the quintet form with which we, amazed to learn of these previous incarnations, are familiar. One reason why third time was in this case the lucky time is that the piano quintet as a medium is naturally suited to musical expression of a rather bold and sweeping expression – the symphonic view of chamber music, so to speak. For Brahms's work is of a type with Schumann's in this respect. Its whole aspect is physically vital and exuberant, and once again the piano part is full and seldom silent, resembling as it were the orchestral backbone of the structure.

Clearly this sort of musical aim does suit the piano quintet as a medium, for César Franck's quintet, though totally individual in expression and design (no obvious parallels with Schumann or Brahms there) does all the same share with them a bigness in concept, being devised with maximum luxurious sonority in mind and most skilfully written in this respect. A symphonic ideal seems to underlie the musical thinking through and through.

The odd man out in this quartet of quintets is Dvořák in A major, chronologically the last. This alone is firmly located on the near-side of my watershed, being entirely chamber music in character, the piano part often rather delicately written, and the expression charming and sunny, not large and commanding.

So at the very moment when I seem on the verge of concluding that piano quintets are best written only by those capable of large, proud and brilliant concepts, along comes Dvořák to show that something much more relaxed can be quite as taking. It may not have appeared so with my own quintet just now, but it was the more relaxed kind of piece I was aiming for. On that Accelerato slowly approaching Ancona 25 years ago, I admit to feeling far more ambitious.

Source: 'Interval Talk' (recorded 6th March 1975)[1]

∞

Stephen Dodgson wrote two piano quintets. No. 1, a work in four movements, dates from 1966, while No. 2, in three movements was composed in 1999. Both were recorded by Emma Abbate and the Tippett Quartet for Toccata Classics (2017). The early piano quartet mentioned at the start of the essay remains withdrawn. The Piano Quintet No. 1 was commissioned by the Battle Festival in Sussex to commemorate the 900th anniversary of the Norman Conquest. In 2000, the composer wrote:

At the time [1966] I was much involved writing music for the BBC drama department, then in its heyday before the debilitating ascendency of TV ... Their task (and mine) was to maximise colour and excitement in the great historical dramas (*Henry VI, Macbeth, Perkin Warbeck, Le Morte d'Arthur*). An intoxicating experience. Some of my evocations of bell chimes and the clash of arms found their way into my quintet in an attempt to evoke that battle of nearly a millennium ago.

---

1 The talk was pre-recorded for a broadcast concert, 'Northern University Concert' from Firth Hall, Sheffield University, BBC Radio 3, 13th March 1975. The concert was given by the Ad Solem Ensemble and included the first broadcast performance of the Piano Quintet in C.

3. On Writing a String Quartet after a Gap of 25 Years

(JULY 1987)

One is always reading of composers who in youth composed lots of quartets, which they strong-mindedly set aside – destroyed even, if they were strong-minded – leaving only their superior later works in the medium for us to admire. Well, I'm another of these. Though whether the later works are superior, I cannot presume to judge. I can only hope.

I have in my cupboard four quartets composed between the ages of 24 and 30; not destroyed, but also not performed since 1960 at the very latest. The first one was a *Fantasy Quartet* which won the RCM Cobbett Prize in 1948, while I was still a student. I've still got the parts of it. In the viola part at one point it says in heavy pencil '... not the tune'. The player didn't know I would take this to heart as a permanent caution. However recondite the thought, clarity of intention is paramount. Your notes should not make it possible for him to suffer this sort of confusion. I think I'm still trying to learn this lesson now.

The most successful of these early quartets – in the material sense, at least of being taken up by a quartet of repute and being programmed quite a lot – was a bold and lusty piece, with powerful colours and a driving rhythm. It was all a bit over-written, and patchy too; but even describing it now revives the excitement it had for me. At any rate the Hirsch String Quartet liked it enough to play it with what seemed like satisfaction. Two others were less lucky in that they were not taken up; a swiftly prepared performance in each case followed by the slow settling of dust. Just as patchy, but one of them certainly far better in texture. And there are things in both – well, all of them really – which still restrain my hand in the bonfire season.

I wrote other chamber music at this time too. A string trio, which is perhaps superior to any of the quartets. And there was a sextet for strings with flute and harp, which the prestigious Wigmore Ensemble frequently played over a period of several years. Though now, I confess, I'm a little surprised at this. The music seems to me meandery and uncertain in direction, though quite nicely written for the medium.

But to return to the quartets. From 1959 to 1984 I wrote none. A 25-year gap, but not a void. I wrote two piano trios, a piano quintet, a second string trio, and other combinations in which strings predominate. What was lacking was never, I believe, inclination. Only stimulus. Plus freedom from other aberrations, like writing guitar music, brass music, choral music and even opera. I've always been ready to follow propositions made to me whenever possible because of a natural desire to provide music that *someone* at least seemed to want. In all of this, I've been lucky in the encouragement I've received; with often hardly a pause between the fulfilling of one commission, and the next already clamouring for attention.

But then one day the stimulus did arrive, in the unexpected form of a Swiss friend of mine proposing to commission me to write a string quartet. He's not a musician himself, but a profound music lover with a special fondness for quartet music. I fancy he witnessed the ventures I was up to and wished to nudge me more fruitfully toward what I'm sure he regards as the Prince of Mediums. He was a little taken aback by my caution, for I was several months in saying 'Yes' – a caution occasioned partly by that 25-year gap. But still more by the special responsibility of a private commission. This is a rare and wonderful thing, which has happened to me four times in the past five years. One of those – from the USA for a piano sonata – was premiered at this Festival [Cheltenham], in this hall [Pittville Pump Room], by Bernard Roberts two years ago. All the other three came from Switzerland. Two, without Cheltenham connection, from the same Swiss flautist, and tonight's quartet from Dr Urs Wagner (who, by the way, is no relation of Richard). He is here tonight with his wife, having arrived in England only today, on purpose. The inscription in my score reads, 'To Urs Wagner, whose persistent encouragement caused this music to be written.'

That word 'persistent' refers to my caution in taking up the challenge, which, if it took him aback initially, he soon came to regard most sympathetically. Once my doubts were sufficiently overcome, I actually wrote the piece quickly at the end of 1984. The Chilingirian Quartet, for whom it was intended from the start, gave it a long rehearsal in 1986. And at the end of it, they amazed me by proposing quite firmly that I should write them a two-cello quintet.

By this time, my chamber music appetite was obviously aroused, since I've not only completed that quintet, but am substantially through a successor to tonight's quartet. This happened because, in the course of writing tonight's, other quartet ideas crossed my mind of a quite other sort, and I resolved to deal with them later. If I was in a quandary before – whether or not to write off those earlier efforts I was describing – my new activity after the 25-year gap has only made it more pressing.

To ease identification, I suppose I shall have to number them some time. So, I might as well seize the present opportunity – before witnesses – to number tonight's as Quartet No. 1 and the one I hope to finish before this summer's out as No. 2. Then those early ones can repose calmly with minus numbers.

I live not far from a busy recording studio. While out doing the shopping, I often run into musician acquaintances, taking the air in the chinks of lucrative recording sessions. A very well-known viola player, member of a quartet which gives a lot of first performances, gave me a penetrating gaze when I told him I'd just completed a quartet. 'I do hope', he said, 'that you've really written it for quartet, and not for four soloists,' and then, remembering I'd said I'd already finished it, added, 'But then I know you understand what quartet music is …'

His remark – the first part of it – completely confirmed my view that if *any* stylistic tendency is observable on the contemporary quartet scene, that pinpointed it. Anyway, I could reassure him quickly. My impulse, I told him, was not only toward integration, but emphatically so. Against the tendency. I was after the power of four with a common aim. The first movement is specially like this. So is the way the work ends. This aspect of the style alone proclaims me a traditionalist.

So does this mean that I'm unconcerned to search textural variety, which so preoccupies others and which is often all a rich possibility in quartet-writing? And if I talk about the 'power of four with a common aim' does that mean there are no passages of rhythmic ambiguity, of metrical uncertainty or expressive conflict within the medium?

Well, I very much hope you may agree with me that such things are there, but not as foreground aims, only as part and parcel of something bigger. As a composer, I am in fact very particular about the spacing and colour of every sound. I never, in any medium, write music in a monochrome and score it afterwards. One of the reasons I love the quartet is that it positively encourages you to be very particular in this respect. The subtle variations in timbre are literally infinite, but they are only meaningful and appealing in relation to the stream of music – if I may call it that – on which they are carried.

And what is this stream in my case? Or, I should say, in *this* case? Because I do not carry over a style from medium to medium, bending the medium to my style. What I *like* to do is to discover myself *through* the medium and not impose myself upon it. I've always imagined that the reason that I've found myself for example writing so much guitar music isn't because of what I said through it; but because I was prepared, eager, insistent that the message would look after itself if I only cared for the medium enough.

I've come to believe too that exploring a medium in the least self-centred way I'm capable of actually becomes the means of enlarging and extending my expressive range and structural imagination. I also very much believe that to search for originality is a pointless endeavour. For me, at least. My argument goes: originality is born in us all to greater or lesser degree. If there is any it will out of its own accord unbidden. No amount of effort will do a blind thing for it. And in any case, the last person to recognise it is likely to be the creator himself.

Even so, I cannot avoid recognising characteristics which have to be mine, and have to be at least as strong as the claims of the medium, since they occur and recur and cross-fertilise between works in very different mediums. This applies specially to matters of structure – which I'll come to a little later. First, I'd like to try to say something about expressive range and intention in my Quartet No. 1 (I'm trying to get used to calling it by its name, now I've christened it). Actually it's very difficult to separate the expression from the structure, because they're all part of the same thing. But at risk of being a bit artificial I'll try.

My expressive ambitions in this work will, I think, be obvious at once in the Poco Adagio with which it opens. It occupies about the first minute and a half. And, as it eventually turns out, everything which happens later has its origins here. It has the seeds of the dramatic flaring up to which the whole work *as a whole* is subject. It has some obsessive harmonic characteristics too. They operate like the hand of fate. The music often seems to be trying to escape them, yet is lured by their magnetism. This is not too fanciful. I actually felt this kind of tension arising as I worked. It is the cause of the breathless gaps which interrupt the driving Agitato which follows the introduction.

It doesn't 'follow' really; more an intervention when the music turns brooding a moment too long and too darkly. The two tempos then fight for dominance but are both set aside for an intensely expressive Andante Sostenuto, in a different time zone altogether, apparently unconnected. But as it proceeds, it begins holding long horizon-gazing harmonies and is threatened with a recurrence of the fever. Then comes the realisation that all this music is related closely in melodic cells, in harmony, in fundamental musical attitude. Yet is left unresolved.

The quartet only has two movements, and this is the halfway mark. Yet, because of what it contains and how it ends, no conclusion is reached. The other movement matches it in length, and also in the expressive idea of an unpredictable juxtaposition of two apparently quite different things. There's another preludial beginning to this movement too; mostly marked 'senza misura', dramatic, recitative-like, as though the lines should have words, were struggling toward speech.

Then a total surprise: a gentle tune over an innocent accompaniment, which goes through five quite classical variations of

The opening of String Quartet No. 1 (1984)

mounting speed, only the last of which contains any emotional disturbance. But it's enough to beckon the dramatic recitative music back, and, once back, it grows more violent than before, though with no more result than to pause and allow the tune and variations back, even more innocent than at first. Three variations only this time. And instead of building in speed, the build is now only heaviness. The last is weighty, but jocular, marked 'pesante'. Unexpectedly the happy spirit is gaining ground. Drama intervenes again, but softened and more tender between its tremolando flurries. Then it subsides and utters quiet bars from early in the first movement. A significant moment, I feel.

My expressive ambition is such that what I hope is experienced here is drawing together all of the conflicting elements – the unresolved ending of the first movement just as much as the oppositions of the second. The thematic material is in fact – I give you my word for it! – all interconnected. At last the prospect is different, the high ridge lies behind, the journey is almost done. We stand poised for a last sprint, marked 'Vivace: Scherzando'.

I tell you another stylistic tendency of today. It is for music to fade away, darkly, inconclusively, anxious and enigmatic. As a mark of my general obstinacy, fondness for running in the teeth of the prevailing wind, this Vivace soon jacks itself into a Presto and ends as decisively as possible.

I said I was going to try to talk about the expressive ambitions of the music without involving the structure. But as you'll be aware I've not succeeded. I suspected I wouldn't for the reason that they're inseparable. Which is how they should be. Expression is only gesture if it lacks structure; and structure is mere formalism if the music is only 'poured into it', as it were. The challenge is how to make them grow together, all through the journey; a journey which of course I did plan and plot before setting out. I knew about the two movements, the inconclusive end to the first, the common stock of melodic and harmonic cells. But how the journey would evolve and be experienced was left to what I can only call a kind of organic inspiration.

That common stock begins to lead a life of its own; which is when composition becomes exciting. At much the time I was in the throes of this quartet, I happened to read – rather late in the day – that very successful modern novel, *The French Lieutenant's Woman* by John Fowles, and enjoyed it a lot. Though was I alone in feeling a little irritated by the author's constant habit of intervening in the story to debate his part in it? However, one of these interruptions somehow comes to pass at this point into my own story – at one point, Fowles felt moved to insert this passage:

You may think novelists always have fixed plans to which they work, so that the future predicted by Chapter One is always inexorably the actuality of Chapter Thirteen. But novelists write for countless different reasons: for money, for fame, for reviewers, for parents, for friends, for loved ones; for vanity, for pride, for curiosity, for amusement: as skilled furniture-makers enjoy making furniture, as drunkards like drinking, as judges like judging, as Sicilians like emptying a shotgun into an enemy's back. I could fill a book with reasons, and they would all be true, though not true of all. Only one same reason is shared by all of us: *we wish to create worlds as real as, but other than the world that is.* Or was. This is why we cannot plan. We know a world is an organism, not a machine. We also know that a genuinely created world must be independent of its creator; a planned world (a world that fully reveals its planning) is a dead world. It is only when our characters and events begin to disobey us that they begin to live.

So far I've not named a single other composer. Now I'll name just one: Leoš Janáček.

On account of those two amazing quartets, which I believe would on their own uphold his reputation even if all the rest of his music were suddenly lost to us. In the second quartet, the movements have their own identifying themes in addition to those which occur elsewhere and which invade them. But even in this quartet there's a strong feeling, as it ends, that it's not four separate movements you've experienced so much as a single one divided into four distinctive but overlapping chapters.

In the first quartet, separation is experienced still less. The expressive world isn't of quite so volcanic a kind, and the individual movements conspicuously do *not* assert themselves with strong themes which are theirs and theirs alone. The thematic material is shared to such an extent that it's quite hard to remember as the music ends, which thing happened in which movement. The whole work has by this time fused into one indivisible unit, the overlaps hiding all the joints.

It so happens there was a performance yesterday in this very room of Janáček's 'Kreutzer Sonata' Quartet ([No. 1]) by the Hagen String Quartet. I'm told they play it with great beauty and conviction, so more's the pity I was not here to hear it. I've not heard the work since I wrote my quartet, but nothing would please me more than to think that something of the response it generates in the listener might carry some kind of echo in mine; which – if I've at all succeeded – likewise fuses into an indivisible unit by the time it finishes.

And if anyone were to think it had even a small part of Janáček's expressive force, I'd be pleased with that too.

Source: A talk given at the Cheltenham Festival prior to the first performance of the String Quartet No. 1 by the Chilingirian Quartet, 15th July 1987

4. The Harp (and Harpists) in my Life

(FEBRUARY 1993)

I can no longer remember the exact circumstances of my first meeting with Maria Korchinska, only that her request for a solo work was made there and then. It was probably in the autumn of 1951, and it wasn't so much a request as an order. She knew precisely when and where it would be premiered: at a recital she was to give on 12th February 1952 at the Mercury Theatre, London (a Macnaghton Concert, then in their pioneering days [and newly revived since a brief initial series and 1931–37 and retitled the New Macnaghton Concerts]).

When she'd had my score a few weeks, I was summoned to hear it. To my astonishment, she insisted I had understood the instrument extremely well and that positively nothing was needed in the way of adjustment. I was of course delighted by this declaration, though knowing full well that the first part of it just wasn't true. I did *not* understand her instrument at all well; I had written for it as an eager novice. Above all, I was overwhelmed to be accorded the status of a fully-fledged composer by so celebrated an instrumentalist, and she moreover famous throughout the profession for speaking her mind with devastating frankness. I was later to hear an example of this, mercifully directed at someone else.

About a year before that meeting which resulted in my *Fantasy* (subsequently published by Stainer & Bell), I had returned from a six-month stay in Italy, made possible by a scholarship I had won on leaving the Royal College of Music in 1949. I was earning my living in school teaching. Though I had won a prize or two, nothing much in the way of public performance had so far come along. This sudden introduction to the harp was encouraging, to say the least.

Maria Korchinska's favourite solo piece was the sonata for harp by Hindemith. It was for her a beacon in 20th-century harp music. She didn't accord my *Fantasy* a place on that level to be sure, but she did insist – forcefully – that it was a significant contribution to the repertoire; and she wasn't one to flatter. In any case, how could I doubt her honesty when she went on to programme my piece far beyond the call of duty, and when she caused virtually all her pupils to study it.

Further proof that her encouragement was no flash in the pan came with her persuading the Wigmore Ensemble, the leading London chamber music ensemble of the time of which she was a founder member, to invite me to write for them. This was *Capriccio and Finale*, which the ensemble played in numerous locations and broadcasts over the next few years. Looking back, their belief in this work was amazing. For me, failures in it loom so much larger than any virtues. But some merit I suppose must have been apparent, for there had been ample time to forget by 1958, when still another request arrived, this time for a duo for flute and harp, specifically for Maria Korchinska and Geoffrey Gilbert, another key member of the Wigmore Ensemble. I can look back 35 years to these four brief movements with many fewer misgivings. Indeed, there's not a note I'd wish to alter.

Between the Duo and the *Fantasy* lay the most crucial formative period of my career, and it's a belated satisfaction to me

now to put on record my debt to Maria Korchinska for the stimulus she provided. The stimulus meant that I nearly always
found a reason to include a harp in orchestral scores, and to take
trouble thinking them out carefully. In fact, my 'training' turned
me into something of a critic of any sloppy harp writing I fancied
I detected in other people's music.

There was then something of a lull in my involvement, though
with just one interruption. At the 1970 Bath Festival, Susan Drake
gave the premiere of my Ballade. This had been specially composed to celebrate her National Federation of Music Societies
award as outstanding young musician of the previous year. Now
feeling a broader confidence in the instrument, I dared to include
quite a lot of linear writing – unlike anything I had included in the
Fantasy, and indeed unlike any harp writing I would now be
inclined to recommend to anyone seeking experience. I saw it as
proof that at no time did I see myself as potential author of a
showpiece. In fact, I believe that those are best left to harpist-
composers themselves. How ridiculous for me to try acting as an
updated Carlos Salzedo[1]; though abundant reason to store up
know-how as to how his colours are made.

It was not Susan Drake so much as her teacher, Marisa Robles,
who illuminated this particular treasure trove for me. Between
1974 and 1980 I wrote chamber music for both of them. Through
Susan I was prompted to delve more profoundly into the harp
as a chamber music participant. I wrote what I thought was
quite a hard and exploratory part for her in Solway Suite (with
flute and viola), and was stunned by the certainty and lack of
complaint with which she mastered it. And in 1980 there followed Ode for harp and strings, with a more rhapsodic and

---

1 Renowned early–20th-century French harpist, pianist, composer and
conductor.

obviously harp-like idiomatic treatment. I have found Susan very self-contained as an artist – everything worked out in advance of any rehearsal I was asked to attend.

By contrast, Marisa Robles had what I at first found the disconcerting habit of trying everything out in my presence while still in a fluid state, probing every note – why was it there at all? – all the things it might mean in the context – what else I might have written that could have conveyed the sense better. Once I got used to this (it didn't take long) these rehearsals became in effect whirlwind lessons in the harp; its technique, scope, limitations and, above all, how to make real music with it. Everything was included as a running commentary on the music – the shortcomings and successes of her students, mishaps at last week's concert, the stature of Zabaleta (her teacher and idol) plus miscellaneous gossip. I would emerge, head reeling, wondering whether she would ever actually learn the *Septet Variations* (1975) she had insisted I should provide for the Allegri-Robles Ensemble; even indeed whether it could possibly be worth her while to do so, the testing and trial of each tiny ingredient being so painstaking a process.

Then came my conclusion, that it perhaps hardly mattered since the boundaries of all that made harp composition appealing had been so extended by the process. Moreover, by the time the work actually came to performance, I had become familiar with the arduous path from writing to performance as experienced and illuminated for me by an artist of remarkable candour. In many small details my score bore tell-tale signs, none of them superimposed, but all evolving naturally from what my notes hinted at but did not positively state. Composition lessons of this value aren't to be had every day, nor do they necessarily come from composition teachers.

In 1981 I responded to a request from two fine American players, David Williams and Larry Palmer, for a duo for harp and harpsichord. Knowing the difficulty of maintaining either instrument in an acceptable tuning on its own, I first needed assurance on this basic point. No problem, I was told; and indeed, I found this to be true. I had already employed harpsichord and guitar in duo, and had included a prominent harp part in the second of the two Guitar Concertos, with the harp sometimes featured as a nearly equal soloist – an effect I was very proud of.

The *Duo alla Fantasia*, premiered in Dallas in 1981, thrilled me on account of the excitements of what was (to me at least) an untried medium. I made great use of the tonal amplitude of the harp in contrast with the uniformity and steadiness of the harpsichord. Its, by comparison, limited compass, its swifter damping and rapid decay when sustained were other factors I aimed to project. The ability of the harp to swell from a whisper to domination is not a characteristic it is much possible to emphasise in a normal duo situation. The harpsichord, however, by its very nature, draws attention to the potential – and vice versa – and leads to a quite fascinating weave of plucked sound. This has haunted me for ten years now, wondering how this particular exploration might be directed. In 1990 I wrote a suite of four short pieces for oboe and harp with the title *Countdown*, which I found a very refreshing assignment, but that other, unidentified perspective remains to beckon me into further harp composition.

Source: Typed manuscript, dated February 1993

∞

Dodgson subsequently wrote his Concertino for flute and harp (1999), *Home-Bred Pictures* for choir with solo harp (2001) and his Duo for horn and harp (2004).

PART 2

Memories & Tributes

Stephen Dodgson was a man who had a gift for friendship and collaboration. In this central section a short series of tributes acts as a sequence of amuse-bouches, capturing personal reflections and insights into the man, at work and at play, his preferred daily pastimes and his approaches to working, whether on his own or with others. The section opens with a more extensive interview with the composer's widow, Jane Clark Dodgson.

Jane Clark Dodgson

AN INTERVIEW WITH LEONORA DAWSON-BOWLING

The following is an edited transcription of a conversation between Stephen Dodgson's widow, Jane Clark Dodgson, and Leonora Dawson-Bowling on 1st September 2023.

∞

LD-B: How did you come to meet Stephen?

JCD: I came from Suffolk and Stephen's father eventually married a Suffolk farmer's daughter (his mother had died a long time earlier). On the whole the marriage was a great success, but she dragged him off to Suffolk out of his Chelsea environment! (He was quite a well-known painter,[1] and he taught at Chelsea School of Art and was chairman of the Young London Group.) And so he went to Suffolk, and his friends and family, including Stephen, used to go and see him as much as they possibly could because they felt he was slightly out in outer darkness! And when I went home for Christmas in 1958, my mum said, 'Oh, we've got a composer coming to tea on Christmas Eve.' My reaction was, 'Oh, how awful!' – I loathed modern music! I got

---

1 Several of John Dodgson's paintings feature on recent recordings of Stephen Dodgson works.

as far as Debussy and Rachmaninov for my performance diploma and I couldn't get any further. Anyway, so I went home and they all came to tea, and my brother, who was always worried I'd end up on the shelf, said, 'Well, what's wrong with him?' I said, 'He's no good!' Three months later I had to send him a telegram saying 'Stephen and I have just got engaged!'

LD-B: What changed?

JCD: Well, I discovered he was rather fun. He really was. He was wonderful. Several days after that, he came to the front door and said, 'I'm afraid you've got less than you bargained for.' So I was rather alarmed. He went on to explain, 'I've just had a tooth out!'

LD-B: He was quite a humorous chap from the start?

Jane and Stephen – a lifelong partnership:
'I discovered he was rather fun. He was wonderful.'

JCD: Absolutely. He had a huge sense of humour and, as all his friends said, he always laughed even more than the people he was telling the stories to. He really did. He'd sit at the dining room table hooting with laughter before he'd even said anything. And he was just so big, he filled the whole room.

LD-B: Was he quite quick-witted generally?

JCD: Absolutely. Amazingly quick-witted. And he was also dangerous. He could say *anything* to anybody. Whereas if I'd said the same thing to somebody, they would have not talked to me for six months!

We had a great Colombian friend called Rafael Puyana – the harpsichordist. And one time he took us out to a very expensive Paris restaurant. And he was talking about Gustav Leonhardt whom he could not bear: 'Gustav Leonhardt – I cannot take it. It is the rhythm. It is terrible! It's terrible!' And Stephen (who thought the same!) waited, then grinned and said, 'Oh, I expect he thinks just the same about you!' I thought we were going to have to pay for our lunch! But Rafael laughed. Stephen would do it with absolute charm. In fact, the French philosopher Fontenelle said, 'Those who are charming to all the world are very difficult to live with.' That's true. Stephen was not easy to live with. But I was just so happy. I didn't care.

LD-B: In what way was he not easy to live with?

JCD: Well partly work and his complete focus on it. Once I came home from taking my aunt from a nursing home to hospital – but she had died on the way. When I came home, I told Stephen what had happened. But he was in the middle of reviewing records for the BBC and said, 'Oh, well, just a minute, I'll just finish this and I'll come.' He didn't mean to be unkind. It was just … I think he was a bit afraid of a lot of emotion. In fact, a great friend of ours observed that Stephen went to boarding school at Stowe and then he went into the Navy and that that had an effect on Stephen. It made him rather bottle everything up. So I think it's probably true. People who went through the war particularly, but he was the kindest possible man. Even though he wasn't awfully easy to live with, he was wonderful.

But if we'd had any children, I'm sure it would have come unstuck because as he said, 'They always have cut fingers or something to deal with,' so you have to stop what you're doing. So it was tricky. And I think that we made the right and good decision because I think it would have been sad for any children.

LD-B: What did a day composing look like? Was there a routine?

JCD: He'd get up, have breakfast. We both would. And he'd go off to his piano at nine o'clock and work away, then he'd stop for a mid-morning break and make salad, then back to work before we'd have lunch. And then he'd usually go out for a bicycle ride or something. He loved taking time completely off between two and four. Then he'd have a cup of the most revolting tea, black tea and milk. (When I first met Stephen, I couldn't believe quite how strong his tea was. He'd say, 'Well, look, that's Navy tea!') Then he would go back, do a bit more. Not an awful lot, but a bit. And then we'd have supper – he loved cooking, so we'd rather share the cooking. And he was very interested in wine. His father had also really enjoyed wine. Stephen was a member of the Wine Society. Actually, when our phone lines got crossed with our neighbour's at No. 1, she said, 'Do your brother and your husband ever talk about anything but wine?!' to which I replied, 'No!' Yes, my brother Simon and Stephen were very close. And that was wonderful. Simon ran the Leeds University Wine Club, so they had a great deal in common: 'Have you tried this?' 'What about trying this?'

LD-B: You say Stephen loved cooking. Did he have any particular favourite dishes or dishes he made a lot?

JCD: He loved curry and he used to make curry. And a wonderful moussaka. Oh, delightful. And all sorts of things. And every Christmas we collected folk who had nowhere else to go. Stephen cooked a turkey, and friends (regulars!) made brandy butter. And I made Stephen's sister Sarah's Christmas pudding recipe and we religiously made his Aunt Syb's marmalade recipe each year.

Oh, and he always made bread for everybody. Paco Peña and Rohan de Saram and goodness knows who else were bread-making students. It was a wonderful wholemeal bread. And he'd experiment. He used to make plaits with white bread. Whenever we went on holiday we had to go miles out of the way if there was a flour mill. I remember going through miles of boring Lincolnshire just to find this flour mill, so he could buy their flour to make bread.

LD-B: In terms of his composing, you mention his fairly firm schedule. How much did he feel that things came to him as inspiration or how much was it him sitting down and actively calling things to mind? Or was there a structure in his head about how to compose?

JCD: I lived with him all those years, but I still didn't understand how on earth something got from his head onto the page. He said he didn't believe in inspiration. And yet the ideas must have come from somewhere. I never could understand it. But he did sit down in the morning, and later there was something there and he rarely changed it... Sometimes, especially if after a performance he felt something hadn't really worked, then he changed it. But on the whole, he didn't. And he nearly always worked to a commission – he was incredibly lucky. He started out just after the war and it was easy then – there were grants and all sorts of things and he won lots of prizes. And he had commissions, so he was terribly lucky.

LD-B: Was he good at meeting deadlines?

JCD: Yes, very. He was terribly professional.

LD-B: And as well as his composition and his teaching at the Royal College of Music he was also a regular contributor and well-recognised voice on Radio 3, wasn't he?

JCD: Oh, yes. And it paid a lot of money, but he really enjoyed it. Even 42 versions of Vivaldi's *Four Seasons*. (That did drive him a bit bonkers!)

LD-B: And across his career of composing, teaching, broadcasting, working with different people, were there things that were particular highlights for him that he looked back on or even in the moment said, 'I'm enjoying this particular set-up so much or working on this'?

JCD: I remember at the end of his life, somebody said something about his views. He said, 'I don't know about that, but I enjoyed *writing* it.' In a way, you could have said he was rather an amateur because maddeningly, of course, he used to talk about some composers being opportunists in that they promoted their music. Stephen wouldn't take opportunities to put himself forward. He'd just say, 'Well they must play it if they like it,' and so his music wouldn't necessarily be known about, and it sat up there in the cupboard. Until after he died. Whereas his friend Joseph Horowitz was always keeping an eye out for spots for his music. And I just wish Stephen had been like that. But he just wasn't.

I used to say all sorts of things like, 'Couldn't we get this out of the cupboard?' In fairness, he was always straight on to the next thing. So there was always something going on... But actually, the day before he died, with all his dementia, he did suddenly say, 'We must do something about *Margaret Catchpole*' [his four-act chamber opera].

I lived with that on my shoulders for two years when miracles began to happen. It started with my friend Sarah Bardwell becoming director of The Red House at Aldeburgh and drawing it to the attention of Roger Wright at Snape. The result was a wonderful concert performance and a Naxos recording.

But thinking more generally about his composition, he did sometimes get a bit fed up with the guitar, even though of course it was very financially rewarding, and it took him all over the place – Canada and Germany and Holland – and he had a lovely time going to all these places. All to do with the guitar and his music – talking about it at festivals and classes and that kind of thing.

And there was a big guitar festival in Hungary. I remember the final concert of this festival in Esztergom, which is the cathedral city of Hungary. The cathedral was *huge* and full, full, full of these guitar students from *everywhere* – all Eastern Europe and Russia. And that was the most amazing experience too.

And the last time *I* went, we had the car and it was lovely as we went via Austria. We went to Sankt Florian where Bruckner was based and then we had a picnic in the Vienna woods with cyclamens all around us. And we went to Eisenstadt, to the Haydn Museum. But this was the era of the Iron Curtain which was a bit of barbed wire – it was right down the Neusiedlersee in the middle. So to get over the border into Hungary, we drove down the road and encountered this barbed wire; and the border guards took *ages*. Eventually they let us through. And they later let us back, of course, just like that! It was fascinating that, it really was. And when we got to Esztergom, there were Russian tanks everywhere. So you felt slightly on edge!

Actually Stephen had learnt Russian at school, so knew a certain amount. And he'd been invited to Russia with Kenneth Leighton as members of the Composers' Guild back in 1960. He went to St Petersburg [then Leningrad], Moscow and Kiev. And it was in the Khrushchev era so much more relaxed than it could be with the Cold War – and he really loved that trip. And he loved the architecture of St Petersburg, of course. And he said Moscow was extraordinary and he was in one of these grey communist hotels, *but* peasants would turn up in the morning and tether their donkeys to the trees outside the hotels and come in for breakfast! Extraordinary.

Wind orchestras were another pioneering thing. Stephen's friend Harry Legge started the Edinburgh Youth Wind Orchestra, which was the first youth wind orchestra (and now they are two a penny of course). And Stephen wrote music for that. He was one of the first – if not pretty well *the* first – composer to do that. And some of his wind music took him travelling.

He wrote a piece based on a piece by Grieg – *Matelot: Diversions after Grieg's Sailor's Song* – for the National Wind Band of Scotland to take to Norway in 1977. He loved Norway but he slipped on a rock outside Grieg's house and cracked a rib. So he said, 'I don't think Grieg can like my piece very much!'

LD-B: I'm well aware of a number of former students who really enjoyed Stephen's teaching – people like the Eden Stell Guitar Duo. Did Stephen talk much about his work with students and teaching them?

JCD: He enjoyed his teaching at the Royal College. He was very interested in the students. He really believed, as his father did – his father was a good teacher – that the one thing he was teaching people was to be themselves. That you mustn't impose anything on them. You've just got to bring out what's there.

And generally, Stephen was also aware of new composers – aware of everything. Admiring what he admired and disliking what he disliked. Actually, he could sometimes be rather high-handed. I remember one wonderful time, when Stephen announced, 'Oh, Kurt Weill is terrible,' Julian Pike, who was a student at the RCM at that time and went on to be Head of Voice at Birmingham Conservatoire, came back with, '*You* don't like it, but it's not terrible.' Julian was right – it is a matter of personal taste. A difference of opinion. Stephen also hated Mahler and loved Bruckner. He thought Mahler was Freudian. He couldn't bear anything faintly Freudian.

LD-B: In what way Freudian?

JCD: Well, introspective and… depressive – he couldn't stand it. And he couldn't stand it in other people. He was very unsympathetic: 'Oh, can't he snap out of it?!' which wasn't always so easy. He wasn't necessarily able to deal with emotions. And yet he got on with my brother fine. My brother had a rather posh botanical career and he did it on lithium – the anti-depressant drug and had to go for regular check-ups. But the funny thing is, Stephen was more understanding with Simon. Personal fondness and affection perhaps.

LD-B: My impression is also that Stephen was good at immediately engaging with people and making friends?

JCD: Absolutely. He was a loyal friend too. People often actually took advantage of him. He was very gullible. And he grew to rely on what he called my 'red light', when I'd say 'no' gently. I watched him being taken in by these people. Some people followed him round or took advantage of him musically – people wanting to be involved with somebody famous which Stephen didn't need.

LD-B: Speaking of fame, awareness of Stephen's work fluctuated during his life. Sometimes he was very well known and sometimes he wasn't. Did that bother him at all or did he not mind?

JCD: It must have done. He didn't let on too much, but it must have done. I'm sure it did. But it was partly his own reluctance, as I say.

LD-B: We know Stephen was a great cook. Am I right in thinking he was quite a gardener as well?

JCD: He was. He had a huge vegetable patch in our garden. And he grew spinach and salads and leeks. He had a great leek competition, always, with our lovely Portuguese cleaner's husband – gardener rivalry over the leeks. They'd say, 'Oh, mine's bigger than yours!' – it was hilarious. And Stephen and I often stayed in a village in France where there was a lovely walk above some vegetable gardens. And everything had to be compared to Stephen's vegetables! But one awful year, I weeded all the leeks up because I was weeding the garden. And they looked like grass. That was not very good idea. That did not go down at all well! But the vegetable garden was always flourishing. And lovely spinach and chard and all sorts of things. And he'd be out there every Sunday morning. Never another time.

LD-B: So that was a strict routine. Was he a man of strong routine generally, do you think? Did he need routine?

JCD: I think so. I don't know if he needed it or created it... I think he needed it. Yes.

LD-B: And did he ever struggle or lose focus when he was composing?

JCD: No, I don't think so. I think he had amazing powers of concentration and he would always say, 'You ought to be able to stop and answer the phone.' And he wouldn't ever let us put the answer phone on. He answered the phone all the time. He could switch out and switch back in again.

And yet when we went for a holiday, you wouldn't know he wrote music. We rarely went to anything musical. We'd go off in the car and go as far as Italy or Switzerland or wherever. And if we were away somewhere, anywhere, and there was an art

Stephen Dodgson happily at work in his garden

gallery, we'd go. Somewhere like Colmar for instance with the famous Isenheim altarpiece.

LD-B: Do you think when you were on holiday, he was almost escaping what was, I suppose, his daily life?

JCD: Quite likely. Yes. He knew Florence backwards. He'd been there with his parents. And if we were in Paris he'd love going to the Louvre. He was very keen on looking at paintings as a form of relaxation. He certainly didn't find music relaxing to go to, but we did have friends who were members of Glyndebourne, so we used to go every year. The four of us with a picnic. But opera was a bit different, actually. He would go. And he loved Verdi – he had a passion for Verdi. So we used to go to wherever Verdi was on. And my first experience of opera was *with* Stephen at Covent Garden. Verdi's *Don Carlos* with Boris Christoff and Grace Bumbry and all these amazing singers. The Visconti production.

LD-B: So he was able to relax and enjoy opera and not be on duty but with other music concerts he somehow...?

JCD: Yes. He did go to the Royal Festival Hall and things, but wouldn't attend concerts when we were on holiday. In England he would go specifically to hear some particular conductor or something he wanted to hear, go to the Festival Hall.

But he wouldn't deviate to go to a symphony concert in Paris if he were down the road in Fontainebleau. That said, we used to stay with Philip and Ursula Jones in Switzerland. Ursula was Swiss. And they occasionally took us to the Lucerne Festival, which Ursula's father had helped to found. And have I told you about getting Stephen into a suit? I said to Stephen that if we were going to Lucerne for Philip, he had to have a suit. 'I don't want a suit!' came the reply! So I countered, 'I don't care what you want! *Philip* will want that.' 'I'm not having a suit!' So I said, 'You *must*.' 'No. A nice jacket and tie will do.' Well one day he went off on his bicycle, as he often did, and he came back with two *enormous* parcels, went upstairs and came back down with the most beautiful suit. So I said, 'Good Lord!'; he firmly answered, 'This is *not* a suit! They came from different parts of the shop. Different hangers.' And where had it come from, I asked? 'Hammersmith Co-op!' And so at the Lucerne Festival Philip, rather surprised, said 'Stephen, that's a lovely suit. Where did you get it?' 'Hammersmith Co-op' echoed round Lucerne!

LD-B: Why was he so against getting a suit?!

JCD: I've no idea! Maybe it was because he suffered a demob suit when he came out of the Navy. They all had these awful demob suits and his was terrible. Maybe it put him off the whole idea.

The one exception was Glyndebourne. He would wear a dinner jacket for Glyndebourne if he had to. But that was a dinner jacket anyway, not a suit. He would conduct in tails because there wasn't any constriction.

And it was also on a slightly drunken picnic with the Joneses up on the high Alps that Philip Jones said, 'Stephen, I can't get any decent arrangements for my brass ensemble. Could you write some?' And I said, 'Well, you should arrange some Scarlatti sonatas. Several were based on band music.' That was my Scarlatti contribution because I knew all about the folk music having played for a Spanish folk dance group and learnt all about Scarlatti from Latin music outwards, and Stephen was fascinated by that. But no – 'No, I've done enough arrange-ments!' That was that – poor Philip! But about six months later Stephen wandered into my room: 'Can I borrow some Scarlatti and have a tinkle?' And he wrote these arrangements, which Philip recorded – quite a lot of them – and they are *fantastic*. They bring out something in that music that you'd never guess was there. It's really amazing. I know every note of them. And they just take off to another level. The original music is still there, but you could never do it with the harpsichord. It's just the vision of the potential.

We also often used to go on holiday with my brother Simon and his wife Ann. Simon was into medieval architecture and Stephen loved that. Absolutely loved it. So the bargain was that Stephen and I learnt Spanish, and Ann and Simon did the architecture tour. It worked very well. It was lovely.

LD-B: How did you learn Spanish?

JCD: Going up the motorway, to Leeds or wherever. We shared the driving and the one that wasn't driving would literally teach ourselves Spanish. I've still got the book.

LD-B: So you'd have a book and you'd teach each other as you went.

JCD: Yes. And then we had stories to read. And when we got there I was frightfully proud of myself because I could make myself understood. And I'm very good at bowling in blithely. I did it with Italian, too. But Stephen would always wait to find the right word, the right verb or what have you. And I'd already parked the car, done the shopping and made friends with the greengrocer lady. But he was still waiting for the right verb.

LD-B: So was Stephen a bit of a perfectionist, would you say?

JCD: Oh, absolutely. Definitely. Yes. Obviously about music, but about language… curry… bread… He was definitely a perfection-ist. And I think that's why he loved François Couperin. He really adored Couperin. He didn't know any of course until I appeared on the scene, but he really took to it. It was extraordinary. In fact, I think we talked about a common idea – a theme – Couperin referenced in his last Ordre portraying a 'winged ass' bewailing his position, in this case not being fed, having parallels to GK Chesterton's donkey's take on entering Jerusalem – one of the poems that Stephen set in *Last of the Leaves*.

LD-B: People often attribute the fact he started writing some harpsichord music to you. Is that fair?

JCD: No. Because he was at the College with a chap called Stanislav Heller, a Czech harpishordist who'd moved over after the war. Stephen had written his first book of harpsichord pieces for him – Six Inventions – before I'd even met him. But he did write one book for me. The first performance of one set was given by a student of mine in the Purcell Room. Trevor Pinnock also played a set at the Wigmore Hall and I turned his pages!

LD-B: How did you come to buy the house in Barnes?

JCD: I walked past it and there was a motorway planned across the common, so it was selling for £17,000. At that point we lived round the corner in a little tiny house, which was rather full with the piano and the harpsichord. Eventually we walked past this house often enough to see the potential. Our bank manager bought it for us. And it was rather a good investment because that was 1966 and it's now worth considerably more! And of course it was good because people could be in the back rehearsing a string quartet or something. And if we shut the door, Stephen couldn't hear it. So that worked well. And then if somebody wanted to come and try something out for Stephen, they could do it in the dining room.

LD-B: So you've always had musicians rehearsing at the house, from the start?

JCD: Oh yes. Always. And we had lodgers at the top. And we used to say we ought to write a book about them. All sorts of people. One was a lovely German scientist. He and his family still turn up – I found them on the doorstep the other day with their two children – this lovely family on the doorstep just dropping in. We all went off to Richmond Park in my old banger!

And we had a little cottage in Suffolk we used. My mother had lived there – she rented it from the Forestry Commission. And when she died, we kept it on and we used to go there a lot and had lots of friends come and visit us. Stephen had a grotty old piano there. And again, he used to work in the morning and I used to fiddle about doing gardening and things, and we loved that. So he became as much of a Suffolk-ophile as I did. And that's really how *Margaret Catchpole* started – because he loved the marshes by the coast and he loved the Fens particularly in winter where *Cadilly* takes place. We both walked miles, also on the Norfolk coast and the Brecklands.

And Stephen and I always used to go out to supper on our birthdays and wedding anniversaries and things. And we had two great places. One was in Ely, the Old Fire Engine House, the other was the Oysterage in Orford. And they were lovely – traditional. And we had various London haunts – when we wanted to go out to supper the two of us on a whim. There was a lovely Cypriot restaurant just off Charlotte Street. We became

part of the family and were invited to one of their wed-
dings, and it was lovely there. And we had another haunt in St
John's Wood, which was rather fun… a sweet lady.

LD-B: As well as walking, Stephen was quite a cyclist, wasn't he?

JCD: Absolutely. He cycled the tow path from Barnes to Reading
or something. In stages and generally alone. And would
get covered in mud! The only time I tried to cycle with him I
couldn't begin to keep up, so no good at all! He also loved
cycling in Richmond Park, a regular time off with a seat and a
view half way!

LD-B: If you were going to sum up the epitome of Stephen as a
person to someone who'd never met him – Stephen Dodgson,
the man – how would you describe him?

JCD: Well really, one of the most typical things is him sitting at
the dining room table in our house with home-baked bread and
relating stories and laughing before anybody else! The other is
going to the piano after breakfast and sitting there until one
o'clock. Disappearing except to come out in the middle to plump
the bread and make the salad. These were such regular things.

Ursula Jones

I first met Stephen Dodgson in the 1950s, after I'd got married to the trumpeter Philip Jones, who was a close friend and colleague of Stephen's. For me, being Swiss-born, Stephen was a typical English gentleman – charming, enthusiastic and slightly eccentric, with a wide range of general knowledge. I remember visiting him with Philip in the Dorset hills in the late 1950s, where Stephen was staying alone at a farm, which was obviously an ideal, peaceful place for composing. We had a lovely time with him visiting interesting cathedrals and sites in the neighbourhood.

After Stephen married Jane, we spent occasional holidays in Switzerland together, especially in the mountains during summertime. Once, Stephen and Jane joined us at the end of July for a traditional alpine festival on Moosalp (Valais), where the cow which has produced the most milk during the summer on the alp is crowned as 'queen of the herd'. This event happens on the last Sunday in July and begins in the morning with an open-air religious service, accompanied by yodel and alphorn performances, followed by dancing and feasting. Stephen and Jane enjoyed such occasions, and we had a wonderful time together.

Stephen composed a brass septet for the Philip Jones Brass Ensemble, which was premiered in a recording for the BBC in August 1957. This was quite early in the PJBE's career, when the group did not yet have many paid engagements. Over the years,

Stephen wrote several more works for Philip's ensemble. Among my favourites are the arrangements of Scarlatti sonatas for brass quintet. I presume that the inspiration came from Jane, who played these on the harpsichord. Scarlatti had lived in Spain for some time where he was impressed by the overwhelming gaiety of village bands. He re-created these sounds in his keyboard sonatas, and Stephen chose these pieces and arranged them brilliantly for Philip's group. They are not easy to perform on brass instruments but, when well rehearsed, are always a big success with audiences.

Stephen, Philip and I shared close birthdays in March – all being 'Pisces' – and I like to think this was possibly another link which made and kept us close together as friends.

Paul Driver

I lived on the top floor of Stephen's Barnes Common house for 12 years. It was a wonderful, generous arrangement – beautiful, quiet rooms at what now seems a ludicrously low rent (and was), and which made it possible for me to survive on my modest fees as a beginning freelance music critic. It was a peculiarly painless transition from university to London. I'm ever grateful not to have been thrust at once into a hard-nosed, hard-grinding metropolitan area. The serenity inside the house and – for all that it lies below Heathrow flight paths – of the 'village' and surrounding heathland, remains with me as an improbably realised ideal of living. Stephen, with his calm, productive composing routine, his unfussed domestic practicality, his invincible geniality, was another kind of illustration of the Good Life.

He was supremely assured as a creative artist. Nothing, it seemed, could upset his methodical industry. He worked, like most composers, chiefly in the mornings, and I would hear the distinctive sound of a piano being 'composed on' – quite different from the instrument merely being 'played'. This was never disturbing, and not because I lived two floors up on the other side of the house. He most certainly did not beat the instrument, in some quasi-Beethovenian transport, into submission. He feathered and cajoled it. He approached the creative task as he approached people: genially and delicately. He used to say he didn't mind being disturbed at his work, because (and it was an observation that struck me) if you know how to concentrate at all, distractions don't affect your resolve, and are even quite pleasant. True concentration isn't a tight thread all too capable of being snapped.

We had countless conversations on the stairs. His knowledge of music was a treasury to dip into, and his personal links to composers and connections within the English musical world made him seem the very embodiment of the latter. If he spoke, say, of EJ Moeran or Anthony Milner or Herbert Howells, it was with pointed anecdote that brought them into the room or hallway. (Howells, admittedly, lived only down the road.) Distinguished people came to dinner or to stay – Wilfrid Mellers, maybe, or Julian Budden, or John Williams; while Andrzej Panufnik, living up river at Twickenham, would send his new scores regularly. I was very impressed by it all – never more so than when asked by the Dodgsons, away in the country, to run an errand (delivering the score of one of his operas) to no other than Joan Sutherland's London address.

Stephen's little library of his own music on the top-floor landing was a rarely entered (at least by me) sanctuary of files and brown envelopes, the accumulation of a lifetime; and somehow, within a quiet house, a place quieter still: as though in deference to the wealth of sound that reposed in it. Another landing-room was a kind of office – it contained the telephone in the days when such things were static objects that rang through the house and must be answered to. I can still hear Stephen's voice calling me down mid-morning – I was probably still in bed! – to speak to someone. His voice was beautifully modulated (as listeners of Radio 3 well knew), and I sometimes think that to lose a person is, more than anything else, to lose a voice. From his I picked up more about music and a host of matters than I can readily distinguish; though I know the general theme was lucidity.

But it's a chat about the shrubbery at the front of the house that sticks strangely in my mind. He was admiring the scent of jasmine on the trellises one summer's day. I'd oddly never been introduced to the fragrance before.

Jonathan Leathwood

The following text is taken from the foreword to the album *Watersmeet* (released in 2005) by guitarist Jonathan Leathwood.

∞

Stephen Dodgson's output for guitar spans half a century and exceeds 40 works. Pieces such as *Fantasy-Divisions* and the First Partita are established classics and his contribution to the study repertoire is as great – and as knowledgeable – as that of any player, though he does not play himself. And yet guitarists who think of him as 'their' composer might be unaware of similar contributions to the harpsichord and the piano, to give just two examples (he has mastered every medium and size of forces). As he focuses on a given instrument he tends to focus, in parallel, on a particular genre: five books of inventions for the harpsichord, seven sonatas for piano, four partitas for guitar.

Dodgson's contribution to the guitar's chamber repertory, above all in combination with other instruments, is the most significant of any modern composer. By responding to each new commission squarely, solving problems of timbre and texture in the context of large-scale pieces, he has repeatedly broken ground in what have since become standard combinations. Works such as the Duo for cello and guitar, *Personent Hodie* for massed guitars (both in this collection), Capriccio for flute and guitar and *Follow the Star* for guitar trio are, in my opinion, unsurpassed in their medium.

In the course of making this album, in which each piece is being recorded for the first time, we were privileged to have the composer listening to every take as it was made. And it is as a supremely attentive listener rather than as a director that his presence is felt everywhere. His prime concern was that we, the performers, could identify with the music at all times – as we shaped the music, it mattered even more to him that we were convinced by it than that he was. He is generous with his own suggestions, sparing in his admonitions and happiest when the performers are excited by their own developing ideas. And identify one must: for although his music is celebrated for its clarity – its pellucid textures, driving rhythms and coolly poised melodies – he can be elusive, too. He is a devotee of the subtle character piece, and while composers have traditionally placed such pieces as interludes within larger forms, he is fond of making them bear the weight of openings or finales. One thinks of the first movement of the Fourth Partita, stark and brooding, with flashes of wildness; the finale to the Duo for cello and guitar, playful but grating and nervous; or the last movement of the Fourth Partita, the slyest movement in the guitar repertoire.

Mark Eden

The following is an edited transcription of a conversation between guitarist Mark Eden and Oliver Chandler on 12th April 2023.

∞

Oliver Chandler: How did you first get to know Stephen's music?

Mark Eden: I grew up on the Isle of Wight and, as you can imagine, there weren't many musical goings-on in the '80s if you were a classical guitarist. But there was this one music shop in Newport, and it stocked guitar music: Walton's *Five Bagatelles;* Britten's *Nocturnal* and other exciting music. I would go there every week, spending my pocket money on sheet music. Then one day in a striking blue cover was Stephen Dodgson's Partita published by Oxford University Press. I thought, 'I've never heard of Stephen Dodgson; it looks slightly austere music – but kind of interesting. It's not lush in the Walton vein, but intriguing all the same.' Something about it really captured my imagination. When I went to the Royal Academy of Music as an undergraduate, Chris Stell and I started playing guitar duos together (and went on to become the Eden Stell Guitar Duo). In our second year,

Michael Lewin, the head of guitar at the Academy, organised a Stephen Dodgson Festival. I remember thinking, 'OK, we're going to meet the man behind the enigmatic Partita!'

Michael arranged for us to play a large-scale duo work by Stephen called *Promenade I*. We learnt it from Stephen's hand-written copy of the music; however, there was nothing which explained the extra-musical programme which forms the inspiration for the piece, just the title: therefore our performance bore no relationship to the work's programmatic narrative. I could imagine Stephen thinking, tactfully, 'What am I going to say to these chaps? They just don't get it!' However, once Stephen had explained the story behind the piece we began to make sense and our performance developed – both within the masterclass and subsequently. Stephen was always honest with students, and very supportive. Later we were lucky enough to go round to his house and play it to him again, probably to show how much we had worked on it; Stephen was so generous with his time. Indeed, we actually played the piece, on and off, throughout the rest of our time at the Academy, along with other duo works, building up our repertoire and concerts experience.

OC: What was the secret narrative behind *Promenade I*?

ME: The audience picture the guitarists, two figures walking along a beautiful promenade seafront; the sun shining. The opening is full of energy and optimism; there are high notes which represent the sunlight dazzling on the water. The promenaders find an inviting place to rest, perhaps a deckchair in the sun. However, their repose is rudely interrupted by a sudden dog fight – loud angry barking chords! The dog fight gets progressively more intense until the promenaders move hurriedly on, the dogs snapping at their heels. Another inviting spot to rest is reached after the excitement but a mysterious mist sweeps in from the sea creating a moment of uncertainty, only for the sunlight to finally break through and allow the pair to move on. The promenaders come upon an old-world merry-go-round, its machinery clanking and whirring, all of these enjoyable sounds harmonising with the setting sun.

Chris and I speculated whether this was a story Stephen had imagined or that it had actually happened; however, being very young students we never plucked up the courage to ask him. It's a fascinating piece. We played it to the Assad brothers [perhaps the world's most famous classical guitar duo] in a masterclass at the Cordoba Festival a year or so later and Odair Assad was really intrigued by it. Every morning he would ask with a big smile, 'Can you play the dog fight again?'

OC: You mentioned that your first impression of Stephen's music, through the window of the Partita, had been that of an austere musical personality. How did working with him affect this initial impression?

ME: I don't think of the First Partita as being austere at all now. It's full of energy, lyricism, beauty and joy, playfully capricious. It is an amazingly condensed work. When we had the festival with Stephen he also adjudicated a composition prize at the Academy. One of the student composers said, 'He [Stephen] told us all to cut down our music: "It's about 20 minutes too long!"' But that's Stephen's aesthetic: it's down to the bone; nothing is wasted; all the fat is taken away. The First Partita isn't austere; it's stream-lined and wonderfully economical.

OC: Tracking back slightly, how many serious pieces for guitar duo were in circulation at the time you performed *Promenade I*?

How much of a rarity was a figure like Dodgson in 20th-century guitar composition?

ME: The Royal Academy had a really good library and Michael Lewin was a font of knowledge, so we had got to know a fair few duo pieces. But in my head I remember thinking, 'Yeah, Stephen's duo is one of the serious guitar duos that's been written'. We had started by playing lute and 19th-century duos, Rodrigo's *Tonadilla,* a Castelnuovo-Tedesco Prelude and Fugue and Brouwer's *Micro Piezas. Promenade I,* by contrast, was over ten minutes long, through-composed with intriguing contrasting sections linked up and thought through. We both knew it was a serious work for two guitars and that's why we were so excited about playing it; it was something we could really get our teeth into. Stephen went on to write a number of other extended duos soon after that time including *Pastourelle* (1992) and *Riversong* (1994), both of which we performed and recorded.

Actually, I was amazed that Stephen never got fed up with guitarists. He wrote so much non-guitar music: choral, symphonic, song cycles, chamber works, etc.; his output was enormous. But he never minded being sometimes labelled as a guitar composer. He wore it as a badge of honour. Stephen was so confident of who he was, never said he should have been taken more or less seriously: he was happy being who he was. That confidence shows in his music as well: he wasn't a follower of musical fashion in terms of his compositional style; he was completely his own man with his own unique style. (John Williams says this, too.)

Stephen's music is all about disruption: he'll set up an idea and then, as soon as he feels like you've got it, he'll cut straight through it with a knife: a sudden change of rhythm, or a melodic line with a new twist. Stephen's the ultimate disruptor. I once asked him if he felt he was a modern-day Baroque composer and he sort of agreed: 'I like those forms, the way the ideas are pitted against one another.' Stephen didn't emulate the urbane aloofness of Neo-Classical composers like Stravinsky; his music is characterised by a direct honesty.

OC: What was it like commissioning music from Stephen?

ME: Stephen was very good at responding to requests for commissions: he'd always make time! We went for a walk with Stephen along the Thames and had lunch with him. This was just post-Academy, probably in the late '90s. We were a little nervous about touting the idea of a double guitar concerto to him, as he didn't seem to be that enamoured by the idea at first. 'Oh no, I don't think that's a very good idea at all,' he had said. After a quite substantial amount of time went by, however, an enormous score landed on my doorstep. I think I sat there for about two hours looking through it – I couldn't believe it! Unbeknown to me at that time Stephen had actually written two other related concertos, a group of three altogether, the others for flute and harp. It was amazing to think that all of that music had somehow blossomed from our tentative suggestion.

OC: Did you gain any insights about how Stephen composed his music from working with him?

ME: Chris [Stell] said that Stephen showed him how he organised his compositions once when he visited at the family home in Barnes. Stephen had said he'd taken Prokofiev's idea of having a pigeonhole system for each of the different scores he was currently working on. Indeed, he'd work on them all more or less concurrently. He might take one out and look at it and go, 'No, I'm not doing that one today,' and continue working on another. I wouldn't be able to focus on *one* piece, let alone two or three! But as well as the works in progress, the room was full of beautifully copied-out scores and parts. Not only was Stephen a prolific composer, but one who was able to find a great musical clarity while working on multiple works and musical projects, as well as creating stunning handwritten copies which I believe really spoke to the performer.

OC: Does Stephen Dodgson have a particular style of guitar writing?

ME: Early on, Stephen was very influenced by his work with John Williams. He had written a small guitar piece at Julian Bream's request in the first instance, and then he'd moved on to the idea of a guitar concerto, but Bream couldn't do it so the young John Williams played it instead. This was back in 1956, and perhaps Stephen then thought that all guitarists could play that well. I laughed about this with Jane and James Gilchrist when we came to record the four John Clare songs – the *Four Poems of John Clare* – which he wrote in 1961: I mean, it's also basically a guitar concerto, especially in the first song; it took me a while to get my fingers around it and feel fluent. As time went on, Stephen changed his guitar writing style to accommodate players. You can see that from the '70s onwards where he got more commissions from other guitarists. In the later song cycle *London Lyrics* (1977), the writing is less dense and there are more single lines allowing the player to be more expressive. Stephen was so adaptable; he definitely had individual performers in mind when he wrote.

On the subject of the John Clare songs, Stephen kindly agreed to take part in a festival of his music over two days at the

Birmingham Conservatoire in 2009. He gave a masterclass to the students on his music including the Clare songs. Stephen was almost moved to tears when explaining to the students of John Clare's unfair incarceration. Owing to what might now be understood as bipolarity, or simply eccentricity, Clare was kept in an asylum because of the conventions of his time. I could see why Stephen was moved by Clare's poetry to write these beautiful songs. Despite its depth of human feeling, Stephen's music is never sentimental; the last song, 'The Fox', captures the brutality of the countryside that Clare cherished.

∞

Throughout the interview, Mark stressed repeatedly the support that Dodgson gave young people: the honesty and kindness of his feedback in masterclasses and informal coaching sessions, and the ways in which he would always respond to commissions from young players. It seems fitting that the story of Dodgson and the guitar should have begun in earnest with a concerto played by the young John Williams, and that the final chapter of the present book shall tell the story of Dodgson's last work: a trumpet concerto written for the 18-year-old Imogen Whitehead (née Hancock). Stephen's commitment to musical excellence, as well as to music in the community, were threads that ran, intertwined, throughout his life.

Anthony Legge

My friendship with Stephen originated when I was quite young, probably not as a friendship, but more likely with a certain amount of fear. I was sent by my father to have harmony lessons with him while I was at school. I was interested in becoming a composer, an occupation to which many young people aspire. But the discipline of counterpoint and harmony with no consecutive fifths was a frightening prospect. Of course Stephen knew that all great composers should begin with a foundation in harmony and counterpoint, and the ability to write fugues; he knew that JS Bach was a godlike example for all of us. So my memories of those lessons seem to have been wiped out. I was also sent by my father to Sir Thomas Beecham's librarian, George Brownfoot, to learn how to write music neatly and clearly. This poor man was made to work punishing hours by the conductor, since all the orchestral parts of the Royal Philharmonic Orchestra were covered in George's blue hairpins on every phrase, in order to indicate Beecham's phrasing; this is why Sir Thomas often seemed reluctant to rehearse, because the orchestra could already see what he wanted in the parts before them.

To get back to the sometimes mad world of Stephen – for an introvert like me, his house in Scarth Road was full of extroverts, and it happened to be a very resonant house; one was quite deafened by the loud voices of the inhabitants. He had a

97

lodger called Michael Steer, who was as loud as Stephen, and they both competed in stories and jokes. I often deputised for Michael on the organ at the local church in Kingston, as well as being asked to go up to Oxford to deputise for him for a pantomime in which he was playing piano in the band; I had to sit through the matinee at his side, only to be shocked to discover the manuscript music he was playing off seemed to have only bar lines with no music in between! How I got through that evening performance by myself is no one's business – it is again wiped from my memory. Stephen would have found it hilarious.

I remember a concert of Victorian drawing room music at the Purcell Room on the South Bank, given by the Parlour Quartet, which was led by Robert Carpenter-Turner, whom I had often coached. I had put on several concerts myself with the same type of material, so was 'au fait' with the repertoire. In the first half of the concert, the quartet sang a trio. This seemed to me to be rather odd as I had never come across that combination of voices in my own research. As I came out into the foyer during the interval, I noticed Stephen surrounded by a group of admirers. Without thinking, I went up to him and asked: 'Did you write that trio?' 'Oh no,' he answered, 'that was a genuine trio discovered by the Parlour Quartet.' I had never heard of the composer mentioned in the programme, but I was convinced by Stephen's clear answer to my question. A few days later, I received a small postcard in Stephen's handwriting, saying I was correct in my assumption; he had written it under an alias to help the quartet find a suitable ensemble, but could not admit it at the time when other people were surrounding him!

Stephen and Jane's house in Scarth Road in Barnes, was, as I mentioned before, a noisy house, but well organised. Jane's rooms were on one side of the house, Stephen's on the other. Jane was the *piano* element on the noise level, but strong in character; she was a fine harpsichordist, and again when I was young, she sweetly allowed me to play her harpsichord. She did remark that through the floorboards she could hear me 'thumping' the keys, as I was playing it like a piano! Only afterwards did I learn from her what the correct harpsichord finger technique should be; no wrist action!

Into this house came many wonderful musicians, amongst whom I met John Williams, for whom Stephen had written so much guitar music, and Rafael Puyana, the amazing Colombian harpsichordist, who helped me fall in love with the instrument. He produced such an amazing rich tone from the keyboard of his harpsichord that my view of the sound of the instrument up to then, as being a weedy dry sound, was completely overturned. [So Beecham was now wrong, it was not a skeleton on a tin roof!]

My father, Harry Legge, who had known Stephen for a long time and who had sent me for those fearful harmony lessons, knew that Stephen's ability as a composer was like the Great Masters of the past; he could apply himself to any commission and adapt his style to its demands. Of course, like Mozart, it helped to know the abilities of the exponents, such as John Williams playing the guitar or Rafael Puyana playing the harpsichord. Thus my father, when he was the conductor of what was originally the British Youth Wind Orchestra from 1969 to 1989, and later under Stephen's chairmanship became a charity and renamed the National Youth Wind Orchestra of Great Britain, commissioned a Wind Symphony from Stephen, which was performed in 1974 in Ripon Cathedral under the auspices of the Harrogate Festival. Stephen magnificently rose to the challenge, as he did in writing a Victorian Trio for the Parlour Quartet, and this inspired Stephen to write for larger ensembles. Later in 1977 Harry commissioned *Epigrams from a Garden* for contralto and clarinet choir, which was performed in the same venue. Now Stephen was ready to write an opera!

I had so hoped I could find a small opera company in Sydney, while I was out there as Associate Music Director of Opera Australia, willing to put on Stephen's opera *Margaret Catchpole*, which has since been recorded with great success. But I was not able to entice anyone to see its potential, even with its Australian connections. Maybe one day …

Thus Stephen was an important influence in my musical life, for which I always will be grateful.

John Lill

I first met Stephen Dodgson when I was an 11-year-old Junior Exhibitioner at the Royal College of Music in 1955. He was my composition teacher in those days and we instantly got on very well. Not only was he an outstanding composer and teacher but he was, and remained, a kind and understanding soul of great sincerity and integrity. His sense of humour was acute and much of our time together was spent in tears of laughter. In those early, headstrong days of mine I tried to write my own piano transcriptions of the Beethoven symphonies and he patiently went out of his way to hear them. He conducted Beethoven's Third Piano Concerto with me at a College concert shortly after – he was outstanding in that capacity too.

Since then I feel so fortunate to have shared such a warm, close friendship with him and his delightful wife Jane. Stephen and I were always amused that our birthdays were exactly 20 years apart and would enjoy celebrating those mutual birthdays in style!

Modest to the core, he never possessed any inflated ego – indeed he was the absolute opposite. He would seldom refer to his remarkable and long list of compositions. He would rather put everyone before himself and remained an unassuming, unaffected man and musician. I, together with the many others lucky enough to have met him, feel greatly strengthened, energised and inspired by his dynamic, warm, vibrant personality and presence.

Richard Field

The following is the tribute given by friend and neighbour Richard Field at a commemorative service for Stephen Dodgson in 2013.

∞

In the 1850s or thereabouts, Mr Scarth the builder built seven houses along an unmade-up road facing Barnes Common. He gave his name to the road and he made the first house the mirror image of the last house, the second house the mirror image of the sixth house and the third house the mirror image of the fifth house. The middle house, No. 4, he made of unique design. It is altogether much grander and more impressive than its neighbours. It is the sort of house that demands to be occupied by a distinguished proprietor and this is what happened in 1969 when it was bought by Stephen Dodgson.

Stephen was not only a distinguished composer; he was also a brilliant investor in real property. He traded up from 10 Beverley Gardens when prices were relatively low and he knew that it was quite unnecessary, let alone wholly inappropriate, to dig for gold under the house. Much better to leave the tributaries of Beverley Brook undisturbed and take one's chances with the market.

For many years, Stephen and Jane's neighbours were Mr Hoare of the banking dynasty and his wife in No. 5 and the Codrington family in No. 3. The Codringtons were a Catholic family with ten children. Stephen affectionately referred to them as the Counter-Reformation. They had so many children they didn't know what to do, and ended up installing at the end of the garden a large wooden schoolroom to get the children out of the house.

By the early 1990s the scene had shifted. There were now new young families on each side of No. 4, the Carneys in No. 2, the Fields in No. 3, the Nitch-Smiths in No. 5, the Newmarks in No. 7 and the Lewises directly behind in 27 Beverley Road. Depending on the time of year, footballs, tennis balls, cricket balls and Frisbees from all three sides frequently disturbed the peace of the Dodgson garden. And thus it was that we all came to know and love Stephen and Jane.

Plato said, 'Music is a moral law. It gives soul to the universe, wings to the mind, flight to the imagination, and charm and gaiety to life and to everything.' Stephen was the embodiment of charm and gaiety. He had an infectious and often eccentric sense of humour. A remembered phrase, a recalled personality, a recollected occurrence, would lead to guffaws of laughter, his eyes shining, his arms waving. He was completely unpompous and free of conceit. I never once saw him in a suit in the 25 years I knew him.

When he spoke about music he wore his learning lightly. He never spoke down to you, and if you paid attention you were rewarded with many insights, amusingly imparted. His enthusiasm was infectious. I remember telling him in his garden that I was going for the first time to hear Janáček's *The Cunning Little Vixen*. He put down his shears, took off his hat, smiled broadly and delightedly told me over the next ten minutes how much he loved this opera for its gaiety, originality and inventiveness.

To my rough ear, Stephen's music is rather complex. 'Smooth Classics' played on Classic FM it is not. I suspect its playing requires the magisterial skills of the likes of John Williams and those whom you heard perform this afternoon. The angelic harpists of above are going to have a testing time.

Stephen was a very interesting man. He had a deep knowledge of literature, film, the theatre and art. At his suggestion, we saw Paolo Sorrentino's film *Il Divo* together at the Riverside Studios, an extraordinary film I shall never forget. But for Stephen's invitation I would never have seen it. We also used occasionally to lend each other a book we thought the other would enjoy. I remember he much admired Peter Ackroyd's *Life of Thomas More* and I have him to thank for introducing me to Elizabeth Grant's *Memoirs of a Highland Lady*.

Stephen disliked the shallowness of modern-day politicians and the vulgarity of modern suburban life. He baulked at the idea of Scarth Road being covered in tarmac and turned into just another urban rat run. Never mind the puddles, never mind the potholes, never mind the dust cart falling into the drain, much better simply to have the road re-graded every few years and a sign saying 'private road'. For a long time the Dodgson road philosophy held sway, assisted by the fact that the lady residents of Scarth Road could not get enough of the handsome engineer who supervised the re-grading works in tight khaki shorts and a short-sleeved shirt.

There always used to be a firework and bonfire party on Scarth Road on the 5th November. These were the days before the tyranny of 'elf and safety'. Bangs and flashes did not appeal to Stephen and Jane, but they cheerfully allowed trestle tables to be set up in their front garden. A hard core of inebriates would collect around the bonfire, which each year became bigger and fiercer. One year we went to bed without damping down the blaze. June Seeking who lived at No. 1 realised that an admonitory visit from the fire brigade was inevitable and turned off every light in her house to avoid a knock on her door. And so it was that the fire brigade admonished the Carneys who were still up with the lights on in No. 2, making merry. Next morning, June Seeking was to be seen in the village sporting an ugly black eye. She had walked into the mantelpiece in the dark. *Justitia eram perfectus.*

Stephen's and Jane's love for each other was an inspiration. He knew, I am sure, how lucky he was to have her as his lifelong companion. They were a single soul inhabiting two bodies. They were inseparable. They went everywhere together. When Jane was invited to teach at Santa Fe University, New Mexico, she insisted that Stephen be given a role so that they could be together. We would see them together in the garden, sometimes planting and weeding, sometimes sharing a meal on a summer's evening wrapped in the joy of each other's company to the exclusion of the world. During the day, they occupied separate but adjoining rooms at the front of the house on the ground floor. As many of you will recall, Stephen could be seen in the room to the left, composing at his piano, whilst Jane would be in the room to the right, playing the harpsichord with great concentration and intensity. They looked for all the world like a model weather forecasting couple within a cuckoo clock, but with this difference: come rain or shine they would come out together holding hands and bearing an umbrella or a sun-shade depending on the weather, these days most often an umbrella.

It was a great privilege to be one of Stephen's many friends. He was a remarkable and truly distinguished man. He lightened our lives with his charm, his humanity, his intelligence and his music. It is so very difficult to grasp that he has left us.

But he will live on in our memories. As Wordsworth wrote[1]:

What though the radiance which was once so bright
Be now forever taken from my sight,
Though nothing can bring back the hour
Of splendour in the grass, of glory in the flower;
We will grieve not, rather find
Strength in what remains behind.

And we should remember these words of Alexander Pope[2]:

Music the fiercest grief can charm,
And Fate's severest rage disarm:
Music can soften pain to ease,
And make despair and madness please:
Our joys below it can improve,
And antedate the bliss above.

---

1 From William Wordsworth's *Splendour in the Grass*
2 From Alexander Pope' *Ode on St. Cecilia's Day*

PART 3

Perspectives on Stephen Dodgson's Work

Stephen Dodgson's output is extensive, covering a strikingly wide variety of genres. Part 3 focuses on a choice selection of them: his guitar music, string quartets, works for harpsichord, opera, choral music and song. It is beyond the scope of this short volume to delve comprehensively into the rich world of Dodgson's orchestral scores, compositions for wind and brass ensembles, piano music and many works for considerably varied groupings of chamber instruments. But it is hoped that the reader will be further inspired to explore these at their leisure.

If Part 1 focused on the single voice of the composer, then Part 3 showcases a diversity of voices and approaches in reflecting on Stephen Dodgson's music itself. After Robert Matthew-Walker's introduction follows a series of essays, each focusing on a different genre. Oliver Chandler then provides a serious and close examination of the details of Dodgson's harmonic idiom that will surely help provide a foundation for future academic scholarship on the composer. Part 3 concludes with a moving description of the composition of Dodgson's final work, his trumpet concerto.

1. Introducing the Music

ROBERT MATTHEW-WALKER

Musically communicative art of such intrinsic quality, craftsmanship and genuine creative impetus as Stephen Dodgson's is not so often found in the output of British composers active during the latter half of the 20th century, the subtleties and genuinely original features of his civilised and inherently undemonstrative music having tended to run counter to the prevailing fashions of the time.

Stephen Dodgson is perhaps best known for his music for guitar, particularly those works written for, and recorded by, John Williams, but Dodgson's output was far more wide-ranging than those – admittedly, greatly significant – compositions. He wrote music for a number of less frequently encountered combinations, alongside several operas and much orchestral music – none, however, on a large scale or demanding unusual instrumentation, although he did compose a number of works for those colleagues and musical friends who were known for their playing of less frequently encountered instruments.

Perhaps it was a combination of excellent compositional craftsmanship, a tenet of, at heart, a tonal-based inspiration and a natural creative communicative desire – alongside a warm personality that was never self-assertive or ambitious – that led to much of Dodgson's work failing to get the wide recognition its essentially communicative and subtly constructed expression deserved.

But to today's attentive listener, Dodgson's appeal goes deeper than the hectoring stance of large orchestras and non-traditional language – his occasional move to the flat-supertonic and the subtly unexpected command of what might super-ficially be termed anticipated harmonic colour reveal a composer in total command of his material, and Dodgson's masterly control of pacing and structure are those of a genuine composer of occasionally superlative gifts.

It is true that Dodgson's post-Second World War discovery of the music of Leoš Janáček was a liberating factor in his own music, but it never descended into imitative gestures. The freedom that the Czech master's approach gave – allied, perhaps to a concurrent, if less ardent admiration for the music of Martinů in its structural control – was wholly positive, lending to Dodgson's freer phraseology and harmonic subtlety, factors which are always germane to the musical argument and never applied arbitrarily.

Together with several other British composers of his genera-tion, much of Stephen Dodgson's output remains unfairly neglected today, but music of such quality, and always so well written for the instruments for which it was created, cannot remain unknown for long. We are not so blessed today with composers of such craftsmanship and appeal as to deny our-selves the opportunity of coming into contact with such civilised and expressive musical art as his contains.

Dodgson's songs, for example, encapsulate – as one might expect – much of the composer's natural expressive language, but an equally significant – and larger – part of Dodgson's output is to be found in his orchestral, chamber and instru-mental work. There surely can be little doubt that it was Dodgson's frequent employment by the BBC and the demands of behind-the-scenes broadcasting that tended to cause his work not to take its rightful place in public or critical estimation. Much the same can be said of the music of Dodgson's contemporary, Robert Simpson: it was Simpson's 30-year career as a BBC Third Programme producer and television pundit that tended to detract from his concurrent serious creative compositional work – any broadcasts of both composers' music was regarded enviously, and unfairly, as 'jobs for the boys': it was not, and the original output of both Simpson and Dodgson suffered thereby.

If one also takes into account the concurrent (in those days) fashion for the overthrow of accepted forms, harmonic creativity and instrumental combinations, such as were to be found in the greater influence of Continental post-war artistic restructuring, it is clear from the distance of our perspective that any inherent rejection in post-1950 British music and music-making of what one might term, in its broader sense, a traditional compositional stance, would have made the output of such composers more readily sidelined through factors which have nothing to do with the quality of expressive musical invention or inherent communicative skill.

But genuine artists can only remain true to themselves: the false adoption of a fashionable stance is ultimately self-defeating, and in the work of Stephen Dodgson we encounter, for our benefit and edification, the art of a truly creative figure, a composer of rare gifts whose music continues to speak with the freshness and vitality that distinguished the output of such an artist throughout his long and productive aesthetic life.

2. The Guitar Works

LANCE BOSMAN

The following is a slightly adapted version of a Stephen Dodgson interview with Lance Bosman for *Guitar* magazine, March 1983.

∞

It is heartening to hear a composer dispel the notion that his art is a heaven-sent gift. True that within every worthy composition there is an inexplicable attraction, an element of mystery eluding definition; but this must be given a context through the conscious craftwork of manipulating ideas and balancing parts. It is this, the extensive labour serving the fleeting inspiration, that Stephen Dodgson can define through long experience and reasoned procedure.

In outline, Dodgson's music is traditionally structured inasmuch that its phrasing is broadly symmetrical, and its forms are sectionalised with contrasting moods. These regular schemes, however, frame distinctive compositions, recognisably his through their melodic and rhythmic quirks. Motifs constructed from these are a prominent feature of Dodgson's music, and once introduced, generate impetus with their expansion and alteration. Offering seemingly endless development, such figures must surely have been carefully chosen, and subject to preliminary investigation so as to explore their potential.

'Often, but by no means invariably. I really like to go at a piece head-on, without thinking too much; but preliminary probings help to build up confidence and give speed and decisiveness to the imagination.' Considering the thought process at subsequent stages, to what extent is the germinal idea borne in mind? Without constant back reference it's possible it could become submerged by the influx of new elements springing from it, hence a break in coherence. 'It's all too easy for me to lose sight of the original impulse. New ideas will keep presenting themselves, and I have constantly to ask "Are they relevant? Do they belong here? Should I save this or that for some future occasion?" On the whole, the difficulty is not having ideas, but having too many all the time. So the answer is certainly yes; it is necessary to keep referring back to the origins; but it's an activity for between-times, not so much whilst actually *progressing* with the music.'

Progression is directed towards, or may even give rise to, an immediate objective and possibly even the distant-end one. If the emergent structure were totally predetermined there would be no latitude for the parts to follow their own dictates or the instrumental colours to be varied at will. Somewhere between the two, a fixed conception and spontaneity, a balance is set. 'Just occasionally I will all of a sudden start something quite unconsidered, on impulse, but usually because an idea of the whole jumps unbidden to mind. It's generally something quite short, happens very seldom and is always welcome. Usually, and virtually always with any more extensive work, I ponder a lot on form, colour, constituents; but modifications do indeed present themselves as one works. It's wrong I think to have too rigid a plan, it spoils the sense of discovery and exploration. But a plan for the journey is essential so as to focus the imagination.'

Stephen Dodgson has written in several idioms, with a predilection for instruments with plucked strings, particularly the harpsichord and guitar. Vocal, chamber music, a symphony for wind instruments and a sonata for brass quintet are also included in his repertoire. Among guitarists Dodgson is renowned for his prolific output of solo compositions, and with the instrument in dialogue with others or in the company of the orchestra: two guitar concertos (1956, 1972), *Four Poems of John Clare* for tenor and guitar (1961), three Partitas for guitar (1963, 1976, 1981), 20 Studies for guitar (1965), *Duo Concertante* for guitar and harpsichord (1968), *Fantasy-Divisions* for guitar (1969), Duo for cello and guitar (1974) and *Transitional Studies* for guitar (1978). A non-guitarist, his association with it is unique, revealing an intimate knowledge of its intricacies. Not only are the virtuosic possibilities of the guitar given vent in his writing, but also the progressive means for accomplishing these from a technical standpoint, through the studies written in collaboration with Hector Quine. Whatever drew Dodgson to the guitar has certainly paid dividends to its contemporary repertoire.

'I don't have a particular attraction to the guitar; but the difficulty of composing for it, and as idiomatically and distinctively as possible, now this is a challenge to the imagination and compositional technique; and that appeals to me. I must say, so does the eagerness of guitarists who have done me the honour of keeping up requests for further efforts from me. I keep saying I'll give up the guitar, but somehow I never seem to do it. My introduction to the guitar was through Julian Bream, and I was never quite the same afterwards. Then John Williams led me on a virtuoso exploration of it, and I was certainly not the same after that. Hector Quine sent me back to school, and in working on the studies, encouraged me, forced me, I nearly said, to understand systematically where previously I had blundered with untutored instinct. Like all growing up, it was at times a painful process; it was almost as bad as having to learn to play the guitar. I say that lightly, but there's some truth, because I did learn to play it with quite a vivid picture of hand positions even as I was imagining what notes to write: that is to say, I *saw* what notes I was writing as well as imagining the sound. More recently I've tried to liberate myself from this; after all, I'm not a guitar player, and it's foolish to think myself one, even at a remove – my technique could never approach actuality. So in writing for younger players, particularly Phillip Thorne and Gabriel Estarellas, I've begun to get back to a purely instinctive approach. And as that's what I'm trying to do now generally in composition, I feel it's a logical approach, and the timing is right; so I'm looking forward to it once more never being the same.'

This then marks a reversion in thinking to when the imagination was unimpaired by knowledge of the guitar's physical limitations. Yet surely these must have been the foremost consideration for the studies? 'I did indeed think about the fingerboard. And in working on the studies, all of them, I thought about it closely, and very instructive it was. But through it, finally, I believe I can sense guitar technique, as it were, organically. When you learn the guitar you have to think much about where your fingers are. Later you have taught them to do much of the work by native response, with more chance for creative factors. As I say, I'm trying to tell myself that, in composing for the guitar, it's time I reached this stage. It's time I stopped fussing about the frets as much as I sometimes have in the past.'

The rhythmic drive of Stephen Dodgson's music generates a sense of lyricism that frequently takes precedence over the melodic element. Another prominent characteristic of his style is the motivic development from uniting fragmentary ideas. In forging these facets, have other composers exerted influence? 'I think all composers influence me; since there is always something to be learnt from those you do not admire – even perhaps particularly from those you do not admire. Those I love, I have to be on my guard against, lest they influence me too much. I feel I can't say anything too meaningful on this one.

'I certainly believe that my idiom is traditional. Not because I've tried to make it so, but mainly because I can't stop it being so. I can't write in a way that feels unnatural to me, and my idiom has just grown the way I am. In so far as I can view it objectively, then in several important respects my writing is in a Neo-Classical style.'

Yet from classical moulds, Dodgson impresses a distinctive stamp, recognisable by particular characteristics, the thumb-prints of his music. Motivic working, in a way reminiscent of Bach, permeates the studies and solos. Urgent rhythms generated by incisive figures surge through, or weave contrapuntally around, the principal line. These figures take the shape of slurred or dotted-note pairs; or repeated-note pairs, or repeated-note triplets. Injecting into, or ending phrases with, repeated chords has the effect of creating expectancy while maintaining impetus. 'My rhythmic ideas are remote from the Baroque. In this respect, more debt to Janáček perhaps. I'm aware of the characteristics mentioned, even sometimes try to intercept them, but I suppose it's deeply ingrained. If I tried I expect I could add to this list, especially as I'm inclined to drive rhythms on other instruments apart from the guitar.

'More and more I've come to think of the guitar as a melody instrument. When the player's main concentration is upon a single line, the expressive projection is at a maximum. Too much harmony cramps the hands, dulls the sound, and impedes the movement. I suppose it's an elementary lesson, but it took me a long time to learn it. The injection of chords – I like your phrase – here and there can be very exciting, and also suggest whole areas of harmony which are seldom actually sounded.'

In connection with this is the personal way in which unresolved discords are implanted to intensify the impact. 'Discords only give impetus where the rhythm has grip; and the stronger the rhythm the more they can give. Where the rhythm is inactive, I find I don't experience discordancy; they are more intervals in space, more or less complex and dense. So the very term discord implies rhythm and drive; and that of course means where does it lead to and *when*? The longer maintained a discord, the more the motifs will tend to rotate, become obsessive. How it is all resolved, or even left unresolved, is entirely a matter of context, and small differences can have a surprisingly large effect on mood and emotional impact.'

Fifteen years separate Dodgson's two guitar concertos. The first, while demonstrating his incipient command of the guitar, is conservative in comparison to the second with its adventurous combinations of orchestral timbre. Written in 1956, the mood of the First Concerto reflects the atmosphere of the surroundings in which it was composed: an isolated farmhouse in Wiltshire. Against this work in three movements and enlisting three clarinets, is the more expansive Second Concerto, now in five movements, pitting the guitar with the prepossessing colours of marimba, glockenspiel and no fewer than three trombones. At times an ethereal quality of sound is conjured by blending these instruments with rapid, though soft guitar arpeggios. Perspective between orchestra and guitar is enhanced by sustaining supporting lines whilst the guitar is busy in front; acute divisions of dynamics; and in setting follow-up parts to adopt the same rhythmic patterns that the guitar, now at rest, had formally taken. A more general technique is to deploy the guitar as a single-line melody instrument with occasional inter-jected chords, reserving its full harmonic thrust for crescendos, particularly in fast movements.

'As soon as the guitar is placed with other instruments, its own nature has to change. With a voice or the flute, provided the guitar is content to accompany, it will show itself one of the perfect accompanying instruments, but the listener no longer appreciates the constituents of its tone colour – I'm searching for the phrase – in the same way as when it plays alone. But the situation changes dramatically again if the guitar seeks to be an equal, or near equal with other more dominant instruments. The solution is not simply the brutal one of writing six-note chords; but how to write for those other instruments in a special way, that give light and air without seeming to emaciate them. The discoveries I have made are: a balance occurs more easily if other instruments avoid the register being employed by the guitar; also, rhythmic figuration is kept quite separate. In writing concertos, I try to avoid as artistically unsatisfactory having the soloist all on his own, and the tutti on their own. This works but hardly leads to integration. When a balance patently does not work in an ensemble piece with guitar, adjustments in scoring seldom help put it right, because it is nearly always a funda-mental matter of the wrong sort of music having been imagined in the first place. I was rather pleased to find in my Second Concerto that a short passage of sustained, slow-moving har-monies on three trombones placed low, well within the bass clef, allowed softly played harmonics on the guitar to be perfectly heard without any strain at all. On the other hand, a single held note on the cellos, if in the same register, is almost certain to force the soloist into playing louder than he wishes.'

With fanfares of repeated notes from the trombones, parallel
4th-chords and rasgueados from the guitar, a kind of early
music–Moorish sound is engendered. Would it be that these
were intended to evoke strains of exotic music in the concerto?
'Not that I'm aware of. But it is modal, certainly. I am always
inclined to be modal; a mixture of them, with intrusive semitones which 'threaten' but do not dislodge them. The Second
Guitar Concerto is distinctly Phrygian, and that I believe is a
great Moorish mode. So I'm happy with your question, but the
thing you detect is, I fear, something impulsive in my
make-up.'

From the buoyancy and lyricism of the concertos, the *Duo
Concertante* for guitar and harpsichord is by comparison,
ominous, its instruments aggressive. The progressive nature of
this piece won favour at the Concours International de Guitare,
where in 1970 it received a joint-prizewinner award. John
Williams, the executor of much of this composer's music, held
his part in the way that we would expect yet, personally speaking, seemed forced into antagonism with the harpsichord. 'It's
recorded very close-up. All plucked instruments always are
recorded that way. I suppose that producers like their artists to
sound aggressive. I did mean a relentless tension, gradually
broadening out at the end into a grand agreement. I wonder if
your reaction would change if you heard the work live?'

A solo work for guitar that merits more exposure is the
Fantasy-Divisions. With a tonal anchorage on the note G, it
nonetheless covers the range of the fingerboard. As to the
structure, the title suggests free-form variations. 'Yes, that's
what I hoped the title would convey. I wrote the opening
Fantasy, feeling that it was a Fantasy, well before the rest; and
for a time not knowing what sort of composition it would
belong to. The tonal location on G is strong all through; and the

steady repeated notes, a feature of the Fantasy, are really recognised in all the succeeding sections.'

The time spent over a composition of course depends on several factors: temperament, the urgency of the commitment, domestic and other musical obligations. Roughly, though, how long would say a concerto or partita take? 'Probably about 30 day-long working sessions. But they may be spread over a period of time, and a good many half-days are likely. I've occasionally kept a diary of a work's progress; this is how I know how to answer the question.' But if the occasion demands, the work rate may be a mite quicker. The accompaniments for three songs by Theodorakis were turned out overnight. 'He used chord symbols – very sketchy. I reckoned each song needed rather constant patterning, to match the mood, and yet give a distinctive quality to each. I didn't sit around on that task. Maria Farantouri, John Williams and I decided on the best key for each, and the character and motion for them. That was day one. On day two I'd finished, for better or worse. It was all the time we had.'

An old man, alone with his memories, draws to mind past events, at times sharp with intensity, then more wistful with moments of sentimentality. These are the images conveyed through *Legend*, a solo work commissioned by Musical New Services for its series of contemporary guitar music. Surges of bustling activity spring organically from two distinct motifs, a concentrated triplet linked to a lyrical quaver group. In contrast, soft and reflective passages are drawn by sustained, slowly moving chords. Besides these descriptive elements other factors, behind the music, figured in determining its length and lending to the mood. 'After several attempts, the piece settled down to a concept of being wholly derived from its opening. At some point, on or nearing completion I fancy, I wrote at the top of the complete pencilled manuscript four lines from Chesterton:

The legend of an epic hour
A child I dreamed, and dream it still,
Under the great grey water-tower
That strikes the stars on Campden Hill.

'Up to that point the piece had been called in thick black pencil
"George Clinton's". Length was determined by the request, six
to seven minutes, all in one piece, not separate movements.
When such a request is made, I'm normally prepared to believe
there must be a need for what is asked for. I tend not to question
it, merely to see if I'm able to respond. I remember the mood to
be reflective, sombre, even brooding, yet with an agitation
within which never really breaks into the open. I see the music
as containing three basic elements: the first six bars, down to
and including the all-important echo effect; the triplet agitation,
bar 23; the brooding chords, bar 33. And these are closely related
by interval and harmony; their contrast shows wholly through
rhythm. The two chordal appearances, from bars 33 and 70
stand up like two solid columns supporting a vaulted structure.
Once this prime architecture was clear to me, the shaping of the
surrounding phrases was a process of motion.'

Accepting that fickle element, inspiration, as intangible,
Dodgson's actual approach to its realisation is through conscious application and articulate thought. His reasoning seems,
as it were, directed from outside the music toward its inner
working. Motivation too, calls for discipline, scheduled to meet
a deadline, or if not, simply self-imposed. 'Even if there is no
deadline of any sort on a composition, I find it a help to set some
kind of timetable. Because, just as there is a rhythm in all life, so
there is a rhythm in composition. If it does not move, it will
stagnate. Sometimes I have to apply the brakes, to stop myself
going too fast, doing too much in a single day. At other times,

when the going is difficult or uncertain, you have to give yourself a prod.'

Which brings about pressures, though not necessarily detrimental ones. These in turn arouse responses of perhaps compulsion, exhaustion, gratification and even depression. 'Yes, all three; and the fourth sometimes. It's depressing if you're not enjoying it; for if you don't, how can anyone else be expected to enjoy it? The so-called drudgery of composition, the writing-out of the score in a fair hand, well I usually enjoy this bit; it's the real test of whether you have notated it in the clearest, least ambiguous fashion. I find I can never really admire what I consider carelessly finished music; I feel it's so unfair to the performers. And what right have I to imagine that I have

Manuscript for Concertino for two guitars and strings:
'The so-called drudgery of composition, the writing-out
of the score in a fair hand, well I usually enjoy this bit.'

inspirations so powerful that hasty, unclear presentation could be justified. Then I see a facsimile of a Berlioz manuscript – that unstable guitar-playing hothead – so neat, thorough and soberly presented; which makes me realise that haste is a popular myth.'

The objectivity of Stephen Dodgson's views are reflected in his music. Yet for all its directness, the sense of fulfilling a function, its conservative contemporary style, it is by no means inhibited: melody is unpredictable, rhythms are incisive, harmony is freed. It is individual, clear and with an outward bearing. 'I dislike introspective music. My whole desire is for something positive, outgoing and full of life and motion. I agree that contemporary music often does seem tending to rhythmic inanimation, so that pieces which are full of interesting detail make overall a dreary and feeble effect – almost as though they dared not risk motion in any direction in case it proves a wrong one. I think that composers who concern themselves overly with self-expression are always boring. Involving your listener, that alone makes composition a worthwhile pursuit. And if there is only one performer, it is equally essential his involvement should seem to fit.

'Clarity, and rhythmic impetus; well, I certainly value those and strive for them. I find I have quite often regretted putting in too many notes, and virtually never felt I'd written too few. Power of communication lies in economy. It's a question of getting any idea to fill just the right space. In guitar music, I'm always hoping to achieve something pithy and succinct because my instinct says that that is characteristic of the instrument, one of its inherent gifts: to be potent, speaking expressively, at once softly and briefly.'

3. The String Quartets

JOANNA BULLIVANT

The string quartet is a curious genre in English music. With its reputation as something of a learnèd discourse between four players, it has levelled accusations of exhibiting a most un-British intellectualism. Alan Bush's famous *Dialectic* for string quartet certainly generated such thoughts with its inspiration in Hegelian philosophy. The quartet is also a genre that tests the mettle of the composer, due in part to the weight of tradition, but also in the fact that formal and creative processes are so exposed in the genre. Ethel Smyth, in fact, referred to the string quartet as being like 'an exquisite omelette' in comparison with works for orchestra that have 'so many ingredients that a rotten egg can pass undetected'.[1] Nevertheless, a striking number of British composers have produced at least one quartet of character and distinction even where their main compositional interests lay elsewhere – from Elgar and Delius to Smyth, Britten and Tippett. In part this was fostered by traditions in music education, notably the Cobbett Composition Prize for composing 'phantasies', which begat a large number of string quartets in the first half of the 20th century, and which aimed to inspire something distinctly English musically by evoking the

---

1 Leah Broad, *Quartet: How Four Women Changed the Musical World* (Faber, 2023), p. 42.

form of the Elizabethan 'fancy'.[2] For other British composers, however, such as Elizabeth Maconchy and Robert Simpson, the string quartet became central to their creative work.

All of this history is helpful in exploring Dodgson's works for string quartet: four 'minus numbers' all written before 1959, and the properly numbered nine quartets spanning the period from 1984 to 2006. Dodgson, as a student at the Royal College of Music, was a winner of the Cobbett Prize in 1948 with a *Fantasy Quartet* (one of the 'minus numbers'). Like Smyth, he recognised the challenges and pedigree of the genre, calling it the 'Prince of Mediums'.[3] In his 1987 talk reproduced in this volume, 'On Writing a String Quartet after a Gap of 25 Years', Dodgson reflected on his dissatisfaction with his early, 'patchy' quartets, but also gave as the primary reason for the hiatus a lack of 'stimulus' in the face of 'a natural desire to provide music that *someone* at least seemed to want'.

Before turning to the nine mature quartets individually, it is worth spending a moment with Dodgson's criticisms of the minus numbered quartets and his strategies in returning to the genre. Regarding the provision of music that 'someone at least seemed to want', we might emphasise the composer's consideration of players. He sought to buck the 1980s trend of writing not for quartet but for four soloists: 'I was after the power of four with a common aim,' he said in 1987. Writing 'gratefully' for performers, as Britten once put it, was thus important, but not at the expense of formal or expressive aims. In his own analysis of String Quartet No. 1, Dodgson points to its

---

2 See David Maw, 'Phantasy Mania: Quest for a National Style' in Emma Hornby and David Maw (eds.), *Essays on the History of English Music in Honour of John Caldwell* (Boydell Press, 2010), pp. 97–121.

3 Stephen Dodgson, 'On Writing a String Quartet After a Gap of 25 Years', this volume, pp. 47–56.

classically-inspired thematic and harmonic integrity, with all material deriving from the first 90 seconds of the Poco Adagio. Yet if this seems to indicate the creation of rigorously predetermined and self-generating musical structures, the composer also invokes the great postmodern novel *The French Lieutenant's Woman*, in which Fowles spoke of characters and events coming to life as they disobey the author. As we shall see, Dodgson's quartets are similarly disobedient, with a profusion of topical allusions to old English dances, nocturnes, crosscurrents and shadowplay, with four players sometimes 'struggling towards speech', and with structures that frequently reverse expressive tone and direction. Let us now, then, explore the 'life' of the individual quartets.

Beginnings: String Quartets Nos. 1–3

The strategies just described are immediately evident in the first three mature string quartets, which are also united by their harmonic and rhythmic techniques and part-writing. Quartet No. 1 opens by declaiming a collection of tones derived from the F major and G sharp minor triads. The bitonal contrast of these two triads is revisited in various transformations throughout both movements of the quartet. One of the joys of this harmonic tension is the variety of expressive moods that it engenders. In the opening movement, the first declamation is followed by stretto entries of rising fast triplets that generate false relations, evoking something of the 'broken' English pastoral tone that can be heard in Vaughan Williams, Ireland and later composers. This emerges, in a very different form, in the bleak Andantino semplice of the second movement from the combination of circular F minor quavers in the second violin beneath a G sharp minor melody in the first violin (Example 1).

Example 1: String Quartet No. 1, mvt. 2, Fig. 25

In yet another expressive alteration, at Fig. 31, the same combination of forces in a new tempo produces briskness and then playfulness between the instruments. The two movements also explore another tension, that encompasses tempo, theme and rhythm. In both movements, initial sections that are variously slow, recitative-like or unmeasured return repeatedly to disrupt sections that are faster, more playful and more energetic. The effect can be haunting, as in the 'senza misura' of the first movement in which the first violin and cello sustain a B-C sharp dyad (two notes played either together or in sequence) against rapid semiquavers in the muted second violin and viola. What these alternations also do is present a clash of temporalities in the work, between moments of progress and moments of inescapable stasis. This, in particular, will prove a theme throughout Dodgson's quartet oeuvre.

The Second String Quartet, indeed, again presents us with contrasting temporalities, but in this case between the cello and three other parts at the outset. The spiccato cello melody of the first movement, endlessly repeated and varied, is echoed and expanded in the answering statements of the violins and violas, overlapping, but never meeting. This brief movement of unified expression opens what will become a quartet-type revisited in the Fourth and Sixth Quartets: a Baroque suite of lighter, often dance-like movements rather than the more traditional selection of dramatic and lyrical movements in the other quartets. In the second movement – 'Andante piacevole' – two temporal and expressive planes are again contrasted: the serene, almost Dowland-like, counterpoint of violins and cello is contrasted by a folk-like 'rough and mischievous' viola part. The third movement is a furious Bartókian dance propelled by cross-rhythms and hemiolas, interspersed with suspenseful moments of sudden stasis. And, on the topic of the Hungarian composer, the 'Nocturne' bears little resemblance to Field and Chopin beyond its triple metre, but perhaps owes something more to Bartók's evocation of night-time natural sounds in his 1926 movement 'Musique nocturnes' from the suite *Out of Doors*. Following a furious 'Capriccio', the final 'Alla danza' is both eclectic and integrative. Dance allusions range from the French Baroque to 1920s elegance, while the conflicts of motion and stasis, serenity and mischief, that marked the earlier movements are all revisited here.

While Dodgson invoked Janáček as inspiration for the First Quartet, it is perhaps the opening of Dodgson's Third Quartet that evokes Janáček's 'Kreutzer Sonata' (String Quartet No. 1) in particular, with the combination of austere passagework and fleeting moments of Romantic passion (Example 2).

The opening chord – CEGB – creates a tonal ambiguity (C major? E minor?) and profusion of fourths and fifths in both melody and harmony that lasts until the movement's final bars, where it is only slightly relieved by the *tierce de Picardie* E major ending. The contemplative English pastoral tone emerges again here – as in the memorable passage of ascending parallel fifths

Example 2: String Quartet No. 3, mvt. 1, bars 7–10

at Fig. 11. In general, the movement's alternation of energetic, but non-directed passagework and such moments of quiet and stasis gives the effect of a fragment of a larger, unending whole. The scherzo second movement is built on the same tonal collection, but is a lighter dance movement, variously elegant and rustic, and propelled by continual metric displacement. The perpetual tremolando of the third movement gives it an almost orchestral atmosphere, like a Sibelius tone poem. As John Warrack has observed, the multisectional finale displays a 'wide range of invention' with the opening material, before a Vivacissimo E major ending.[4]

---

4 John Warrack, liner notes to *Stephen Dodgson: String Quartets, Volume II*, The Tippett Quartet, Dutton Epoch CD, CDLX 7182 (2008).

Pastiche: String Quartets Nos. 4–6

The middle three mature quartets offer features we have seen before – allusions to the Baroque suite, contemplative parallel fifths, a sense of discourse between players – but there is also a departure here in terms of even greater assurance and sense of form within movements. The Fourth Quartet, like the second, is a suite of diverse movements with evocative titles. The opening 'Colloquy' establishes a basic melodic line, like a fugue subject, that is then broken up and varied contrapuntally to create a tautly thematic movement. The second movement, 'Play', is playful in various senses. The pervasive dotted-semiquaver theme is light-hearted in itself, but the movement also 'plays' with its material, seeking ever new combinations of the note collection first heard in full in bar 3. The third movement 'Shadowplay' is more enigmatic in meaning, and it again evokes something of Bartók's night music. However, the similarities of thematic material with 'Play', reset as ghostly harmonics, could also support an understanding of the movement as a 'shadow' of its predecessor. The 'Canzona' is a sectional movement of exquisite contrapuntal part-writing and lyrical beauty. The final 'Alla danza' is a restrained, Neo-Classical dance, with rhythmic and tonal gestures subtly subverted to avoid any conventional sense of resolution.

The Fifth Quartet returns to abstraction, but with the same energy and mastery of part-writing that characterised the Fourth. The opening 'Con brio' establishes a familiar strategy – the juxtaposition of passages of music with contrasting characters and temporalities. This eventually coalesces into passages of *leggiero* contrapuntal triple metre set against suspenseful homophonic sections in an irregular 7/4 metre, but the latter is actually present, implicitly, from the opening. The whole Fifth Quartet has a lightness and brevity that contrasts with the intensity of some of the earlier quartets. The 'Tranquillo' slow movement is another exercise in night music, in its combination of slow, sustained melody with bursts of rapid passagework, yet it is also warmer than comparable movements like 'Shadowplay'. The final 'Non troppo vivace; con forza' has moments of force, but also of delicacy and song-fulness. As a whole, the Quartet gives the impression of transient pleasure.

The Sixth Quartet is the last in the style of the Baroque suite and the one which is most consistently faithful to that model. The opening 'Arioso' is preludial and invocatory; the rising fourths and 'senza misura' marking give the effect of sunrise and birdsong. The 'First Dance' alternates a rapid, triple-metre courante with passages of what might be considered the partnering stately allemande. The latter sections, however, also have a hymn-like quality, as well as a strong note of nostalgia in the combination of largely functional harmony with a soaring, ghostly first violin counter-melody. The 'Second Dance', by contrast, is a stately sarabande, replete with the ornamentation that gave the Baroque its name. The 'Recitative and Ground' return us to a world of speech and song in the lyrical viola solo that emerges above the cello's ground bass – a rare instance in Dodgson's quartets of a single instrument taking centre-stage throughout a movement. The name of the 'Caccia' evokes a hunt, although the musical form was con-ventionally a two-voice canon. Dodgson's 'Caccia' initially gives the impression of a canon without strictly adhering to the principle. Thereafter, as in the Third Quartet, the finale proceeds through contrasting, endlessly inventive sections to a light-hearted Presto conclusion.

Neo-Classicism: String Quartets Nos. 7–9

String Quartet No. 7 has the moniker 'Cross-currents', a title that may refer variously to the evocation of flowing water or the broader patterns of rhythmic and contrapuntal contrast that characterise the work. The first movement – 'Sustained and Quietly Flowing' – is almost minimalist in texture, with much of the initial section a seemingly infinite dialogue of semiquavers between second violin and cello. Nevertheless, the interjections of the other instruments gradually intensify up to the sudden shift to *pianissimo* unison quavers at bar 53. While the flowing semiquavers resume, the end of the movement is a synthesis of the rhetoric of the unison quavers and the melodic profile of the flowing, alternating second violin/cello theme. The second movement demonstrates the quartet's 'polarities of stasis and kinetic energy', as Peter Palmer has observed.[5] The opening outlines, very simply, two dyads in counterpoint (Example 3), which by a process of developing variation weaves a series of themes of the movement, variously producing flowing, descending semiquaver perpetual motion and jagged ascending patterns which disrupt the flow. The third movement recalls the 'Second Dance' of the Sixth Quartet with its stately, highly ornamented themes. The finale faithfully evokes the stated 'Strength and Turbulence opposed to a Dancing Lightness', alternating an impassioned melody in common time featuring metrical displacement with sections of regular, dance-like triple metre, leading to the variety of expressive character that is so prominent in Dodgson's final movements.

---

5 Peter Palmer, 'CD Reviews', *Tempo* Vol. 61 No. 242 (2007), pp. 78–9.

Example 3: String Quartet No. 7, mvt 2, bars 1–6

String Quartet No. 8 is, as John Warrack observes, a 'compact and charged work'.[6] The first movement begins with a 'Bright and Purposeful' refined Neo-Classical counterpoint in E flat. Passages in this style are juxtaposed with passages of tranquil English homophony, in which Dodgson uses the E flat/D sharp enharmonic equivalence to explore keys around B major. While remaining in strict time, the mournful melodies of the middle movement recall something of the rhapsodic folk-like

6 John Warrack, liner notes to *Stephen Dodgson: String Quartets. Volume III*, The Tippett Quartet, Dutton Epoch, CDLX 7265 (2008).

character found in the early quartets. Like the finale of Britten's Second String Quartet (1945), the final movement is a strict and intense chaconne, though with more immediate expressive variety than Britten's slow-burning movement. The 13-bar basis of the chaconne is a contrapuntal harmonic-melodic complex distributed among the instruments and continuously varied. The ending of the quartet is sudden and muted, as if the infinite cycles of variation were merely suspended rather than resolved.

The Ninth Quartet, fittingly, displays many of the characteristic techniques and modes of expression refined through its predecessors. The opening 'Andante' ranges between the evocative intensity of the first three quartets and the stylised *leggiero* of Dodgson's Neo-Classical writing. The 'Animato' deploys pizzicato as an integral feature to an extent not seen before in his oeuvre. The third movement is one final piece of night music, with ephemeral sounds flitting around a sustained melodic core. The heart of the piece is ecstatic in tone and intensity. In the final movement, one is reminded of Britten's music once again with the presence of a march that subverts the rhetoric of a march, constantly alternating the typical common time with triple-time music of – as in the Seventh Quartet – a dancing lightness. Appropriately, then, Dodgson's quartet cycle ends with the same reinvention of old forms, expressive and temporal contrasts, and exquisite string writing with which it began. The quartets show remarkable consistency of procedure, but also ever-increasing assurance in the medium, combined with the ability to explore new models and procedures even into the finale of the Ninth. Perhaps, like John Fowles, Dodgson indeed allowed these works to take on a life of their own.

Stephen, aged 2, at Dymchurch, summer of 1926, and
in London with his sisters, Ann and Sarah, in 1927.

Stephen (left) with first-cousins-once-removed
Bic and Bill Pease, circa 1934.

At the wedding of cousin Bridie in 1945: Left to right: Stephen's parents John and Margaret ('Val') Dodgson, first-cousin-once-removed Bill Pease, sister Ann, uncle Seton Gordon (father of the bride), family friend Olive Maitland and Stephen.

Stephen with niece Lindie, circa 1955.

Jane and Stephen on their wedding day, 23rd July 1959.

Left: John Dodgson and sister 'Aunt Sybil'.
Right: Agnes, John's second wife, Stephen's stepmother.

Stephen at the farmhouse in Hippenscombe:
'The mood of the First Guitar Concerto reflects the atmosphere
of the surroundings in which it was composed: an isolated
farmhouse in Wiltshire.' – Lance Bosman

Playing through one of his manuscripts.

Stephen Dodgson with guitarist John Williams and harpsichordist Rafael Puyana.

Stephen Dodgson was keen to give support to young musicians and would provide honest and kind feedback in masterclasses and informal coaching sessions. (This photo from the guitar course in Rehoboth, New England, 1976.)

With guitarist Robert J Vidal at the Segovia International Classical Guitar Contest in Paris, 1978.

With fellow jury members of the Segovia International Classical Guitar Contest at Leeds Castle in 1981.

'Not only was Stephen a prolific composer, but one who was able to find a great musical clarity while working on multiple works and musical projects, as well as creating stunning handwritten copies which I believe really spoke to the performer.' – Mark Eden

With composer and guitarist-singer John Miles (left) and conductor Chris Wiltshire (middle) in front of the Newcastle City Hall in 1988 on the occasion of the premiere of *A Country Wedding*, commissioned and performed by the Felling Male-Voice Choir. He was further commissioned by Wiltshire to write his Symphony in One Movement for the Sheffield Chamber Orchestra.

Stephen with *Margaret Catchpole* librettist Ronald Fletcher (1979).

Margaret Catchpole: Ameral Gunson (Margaret) and Jack Irons (Laud).

Margaret Catchpole: Julian Pike (Crusoe), Mark Rowlinson (Luff),
Jack Irons (Laud). Both photos from the original production in 1979.

Stephen in his beloved Fenlands, so
evidently present in the music of *Margaret Catchpole*.

ESCAPED
Margaret Catchpole,

A CONVICT

Under Sentence of Transportation, for

FELONY, AND HORSE-STEALING

7pm Friday 5th July
Britten Studio, Snape Maltings

A rare concert performance of Stephen Dodgson's chamber opera
Margaret Catchpole: Two Worlds Apart.

A LOCAL TALE OF MISGUIDED
PASSION, LOYALTY AND FATE

The opera tells the story of the Suffolk heroine, criminal and chronicler
Margaret Catchpole. We are immersed in her internal battle between her
own good character and values, and her heartfelt loyalty to Will Laud,
a smuggler – the man she loves.

Kate Howden, Matthew Brook, Richard Edgar-Wilson, William Wallace, Nicholas Morris,
Alistair Ollerenshaw, Peter Willcock, Diana Moore, Robyn Allegra Parton, Jon Stainsby,
Michael Bundy, Leonora Dawson-Bowling, Mark Saberton, Jonathan Hanley,
Ensemble Perpetuo directed by Julian Perkins

Tickets: £20 from the Snape Maltings box office,
www.snapemaltings.co.uk or on 01728 687110

Tickets include Anthony Cobbold pre-concert talk.

Granted by Act of Parliament

The night before he died, Stephen Dodgson said, 'We must do
something about *Margaret Catchpole*'. His wish was fulfilled.
The opera was performed and recorded at Snape Maltings in July 2019.

Prussia Cove International Guitar Seminar circa 1985: Stephen provides encouragement during one of his classes. And group shot on the cliff (left to right) – Gerald Garcia, John Canning, Paul Gregory, Stephen Gordon, Phillip Thorne, Stephen Dodgson, Martin Fleeson.

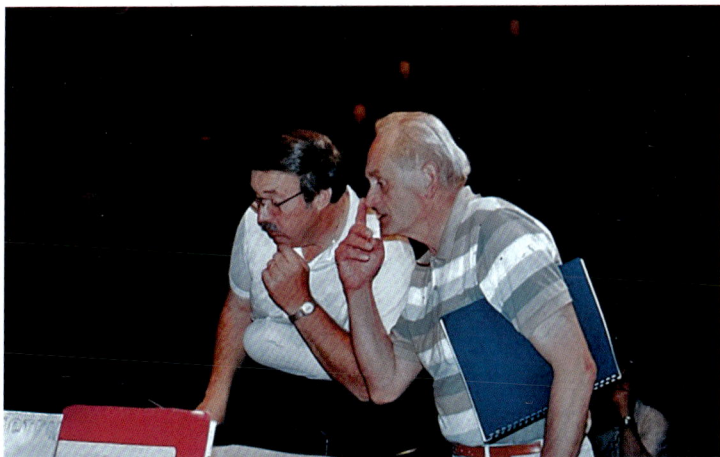

'We decided if anyone could bring [off a harpsichord concerto with an ensemble of wind, brass and percussion], you could.'
Arlington Concertante recording (1986): Above: Stephen Dodgson and conductor Ray Lichtenwalter consult over the score. Below: the two review recording playback with harpsichordist Linton Powell.

The house and garden in Barnes including Stephen Dodgson's study, complete with the desk where he composed overlooking Barnes Common. (The painting, *Summer Trees* by artist Clive Randall, was painted in Stephen's garden and later used on the cover of the Bernard Roberts piano sonata recordings.)

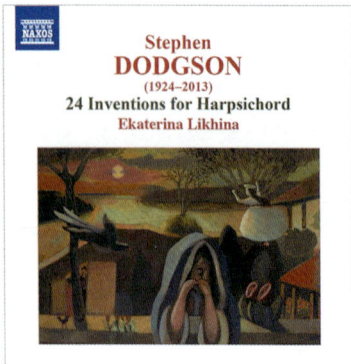

Several vivid and imaginative John Dodgson paintings feature on recent Stephen Dodgson recordings.

Death of a Child

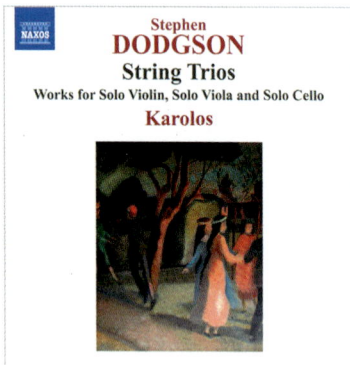

Dancing in the Garden

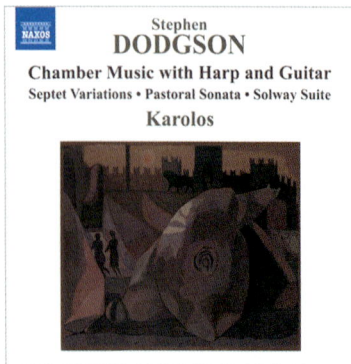

The Giant Snail

Philip Jones, Stephen and Jane having a short rest on a walk in the Swiss mountains.

Stephen, Ursula Jones and Jane at the foot of the Ried glacier.

A proud moment – Stephen Dodgson and his plaited bread.

Facing: A typical welcoming Barnes evening of tea in the kitchen, wine and nibbles in the sitting room and supper in the dining room with Jane's sister-in-law Ann.

Hosting in Barnes – Christmas with friends Hermione Sandwith, the National Trust's first Advisor on Conservation, Henry Pleasants, music critic and former intelligence officer, and John Lade, the founder of the Radio 3 BBC Record Review.

Stephen with Valda Aveling and Evelyn Barbirolli,
for whom he wrote his Suite for oboe and harpsichord
(Friends of Junior Department, Trinity College of Music
'Conversazione' 30th May 1992).

With composer-friend Bill Connor.

Jane and Stephen on an afternoon out to Chiswick House.

Working with the Bernard Roberts Piano Trio, Andrew Roberts (violin), Bernard Roberts (piano) and Nicholas Roberts (cello) on their Dodgson trio recording at St Paul's School, Barnes in 2002.

A Thames-side walk with Bernard Roberts on a recording break.

Eden Stell Guitar Duo (Mark Eden and Chris Stell) with Stephen Dodgson at the Presteigne Festival in 2001.

80th birthday at the Royal Academy of Music in 2004.
With guitarists John Williams, Hector Quine and Michael Lewin.

With trumpeter Imogen Whitehead at the UK premiere of the
Trumpet Concerto at Kingston Parish Church, September 2011.

Stephen Dodgson with the Tippett Quartet at the
Barnes Music Festival in March 2013 shortly before his death.

4. Works for Harpsichord

PAMELA NASH

The following interview with Stephen Dodgson first appeared in *The Diapason* in 2001.

∞

Stephen Dodgson has composed for almost every instrumental genre, his works for the guitar having brought him particular notice. However, Dodgson has also earned a place in 20th-century harpsichord history and he has probably the longest and most productive association with the harpsichord of any living composer. His affinity with the instrument has been nurtured by the developments in the harpsichord world over the last 40 years, and his output now comprises 49 works, both solo and ensemble.

In my capacity as a harpsichordist and performer of contemporary music. I regard Dodgson as a singularly gifted champion of the harpsichord whose works should have wider recognition. His strength of feeling and depth of intuition for the instrument produces writing that is wholly idiomatic; his economy of line, clarity of voicing, control of texture and dynamic rhythmic treatment are always expressed in ways that bring the harpsichord to life. I asked Dodgson about his work with the instrument and about his philosophy on contemporary harpsichord matters.

∞

Pamela Nash: Is your penchant for the harpsichord partly a practical one – an outcome of being exposed to the instrument in your working environment?

Stephen Dodgson: I always seem to respond to its rhythmic clarity, and the vividness of texture and spacing. Perhaps 'living with harpsichords' quickens this response, but it's certainly not the cause of it.

PN: Can you recall your first encounter with the harpsichord?

SD: I can pinpoint it exactly. It was an afternoon in early summer 1955, when Stanislav Heller introduced me to Thomas Goff and his instruments with the definite aim that I should become interested in composing for him and for them.

PN: How did marriage to harpsichordist and Couperin expert Jane Clark foster your appreciation?

SD: It quickly extended my knowledge of the repertoire and this has subtly infected my perception of the instrument itself.

PN: Are there particular works that have provided the inspiration and impetus to compose for the harpsichord?

SD: At the start, Scarlatti was uppermost. Then it broadened out; the inspirational factor has been a generalised one of character, not so much deriving from one specific work.

PN: With the exception of a few pieces such as the Falla and Martin concertos [completed in 1926 and 1952], harpsichord music before 1950 was either a sort of adjunct to the piano repertoire and impractical to play, or it was a pastiche of old idioms. You were one of the first to break these moulds by writing true and characteristic music for the harpsichord: were you prompted by the burgeoning interest in the harpsichord in the 1950s, and by the new generation of players who were pursuing modern harpsichord repertoire?

SD: I was a lot less aware than your question supposes. I just leapt in excitedly. But it happened to coincide with the explosion of interest among players and makers alike. George Malcolm, Stanislav Heller and Antonio Saffi were very encouraging. They liked what I wrote and played it.

PN: You have been an observer of the harpsichord revival from those early days of your career; has your harpsichord music reflected the changes and developments in the instrument during the past 40 or so years?

SD: I believe the evolution of the instrument is actually reflected in what I've written – with the 'classical' instrument steadily in the ascendant. Going back where I began is unthinkable.

PN: Has the harpsichord been a technical factor in your development as a composer? Has it influenced the ways you write for other instruments?

SD: It occupies a place all of its own in my thinking. Which is why I am jealous of being as idiomatic as possible in my approach. But because I value economy of means in everything I write, and an 'open space' approach is an essential factor in good harpsichord writing (in any century!) I'm sure there has been some cross-over influence.

PN: Your harpsichord music is very rewarding to play, the main reason being that its style and idiom coincide very logically and happily with the harpsichord's character. This enables the player to make the music speak easily and directly. How does this work; do your ideas originate at the harpsichord? How do you consider technical things like handshifts and fingering in your composing?

SD: I never take something new to the harpsichord until I'm pretty certain of it musically. I then find I may here and there want to move up or down an octave – and leave out still a few more notes than I'd been crossing out the week before. Handshifts and fingerings can actually be exciting things in harpsichord writing, because they are integral to the result in phrasing and attack. Some ideas have actually originated in this way: for example, Invention Set 5, No. 3 (Example 1).

Example 1: Invention Set 5, No. 3

PN: You also have a very strong symbiotic relationship with the guitar. Your harpsichord music seems to demonstrate how close the relationship is between the guitar and the harpsichord, and some of your ideas are found in the repertoires of both instruments. Do they have similar limitations that you can treat in the same ways?

SD: Of course, harpsichord and guitar must both have their limitations. One has heard music on each of them which palpably didn't suit. But there's so much that can be written on each successfully, I've never found it profitable to think about limitations. Rather, I've always preferred going for it positively, trying to develop an instinct for what will succeed and give the performer satisfaction.

PN: Combining harpsichord and guitar in *Duo Concertante* and *Dialogues* must have been uniquely difficult.

SD: When asked to write for harpsichord and guitar together, I simply couldn't persuade myself it could work. But Rafael Puyana and John Williams insisted it did, so I took courage in my hands, and as I worked began to believe in it more and more.

PN: Because their timbres are at once similar and different, how did you reconcile them, both in off-setting them soloistically and in combining them homogeneously?

SD: The fascination is because they are similar yet different. My object was to make them homogeneous here, and by contrast very separated in other places; figuration and spacing are important factors; how to devise dialogues that bring out different facets in the relationship. Then there was the excitement of finding a dramatic structure to give such colourings purpose.

PN: You often end a phrase with an octave unison or an open fifth, which is very idiomatic for plucked instruments where chords can actually sound louder without the third – for example, the ending of the *Duo Concertante*, where it sounds as though there are several guitars and harpsichords playing! You

also juxtapose thick-voiced harmonies of thirds with open fifths
or unisons a lot, which seems to have to do with accentuating
the pulse, and with rhythmical stress and energy. The notes
often seem subservient to the pulse, as in Scarlatti (Example 2:
Invention Set 3, No. 3).

Example 2: Invention Set 3, No. 3

SD: Agreed! This is certainly something I learnt from Scarlatti.
Rhythmic stress does indeed require additional notes. In
cadential situations the big bare intervals appeal through their
primary force.

PN: Would you say there are other significant parallels between
Scarlatti's harpsichord writing and your own? For example, in
the use of harmonic texture: in leaving out the third of the chord
and opening out the last chord in a progression to an octave or
fifth; the use of an ornament on the off-beat; the tied chord on
the last beat or the half-beat, which gives a syncopated weight
or accent, significantly on the anacrusis. The use of rhythm and
timing to create drama and suspense in the way the music
breathes and is sometimes suspended is also similar. Although
Scarlatti was specifically concerned with emulating flamencan
rhythm on the harpsichord, your music seems to function on the
same level as it too explores the harpsichord's ability to dance
and 'swing'. Are these reasonable comparisons?

SD: Yes – to my mind they are very close indeed to my way of going about it, and you're right to point out my penchant for the anacrusis accent, perhaps with an ornament for extra emphasis (Example 3: Invention Set 3, No. 4).

Example 3: Invention Set 3, No. 4

PN: It is often said that there is an English quality about your music in general. What is it, do you think, that gives this impression?

SD: I think I'm just very English – full stop!

∞

Dodgson's use of dynamics (before Inventions Set 4) is very economical for the harpsichord, which adds to the practicality of his music on the classical-type instrument. He has gone from using standard dynamics, to registration dynamics, to no dynamics at all with Set 4 of the Inventions. A decade later in the

most recent fifth set, all expression marks are eschewed to leave
'just the notes'. The dynamic and expressive feeling in the music
has always been intrinsic, in the Baroque sense; very often, a
marking of 'p' or 'f' is reflected in the notes themselves, in a shift
to a different tessitura, or a change of texture, pace or harmonic
rhythm. Then to add the registration is merely an accentuation
of the inherent musical dynamics.

Example 4: Invention Set 3, No. 1

PN: Could you explain the evolution of the dynamic treatment
in the Inventions? In some of the earlier writing where the
registration dynamics cannot be realised on the classical
harpsichord, are you happy for the player to revise them?

SD: I may have been reasonably consistent about dynamic markings at any one time, but, overall, I think there's no consistent
development. At first I only thought in terms of two-manual
instruments. In general therefore the *f* and *p* invite a registration
change, or an addition/subtraction of four-foot or coupler. By the
time of Set 5 I'd become concentrated on making all the colouring
arise from the music itself, with the ambitious aim that the whole
set could succeed on a single register throughout without seeming
monochrome. In settling for 'just the notes' notation I'd convinced
myself anything else would be a distraction. I actually want to
appeal to the imagination of the player! And this naturally applies

too to those spots where my notated changes cannot be realised on the instrument being used.

PN: Have you also dispensed with the use of accents? In your earlier writing the accent or [–] tenuto dash is often poignant as an indication of the rhythmic intent, or the importance of a note. And although accent in the tonal sense (as on the piano) cannot be realised on the harpsichord, in some ways the spirit of it can be: for example, as an agogic accent, or a tenuto or inégale form of accent.

SD: In general I'm a great supplier of accent signs, but more and more I question their relevance for the harpsichord. I'm also a great one for beaming notes according to their accentual grouping, and allowing these to criss-cross with the metrical organisation. This dispenses with most of any remaining need for accent signs. But who can deny the psychological impact of a *sforzando* where the intention is dramatic? So I don't promise never to use accent marking in the future.

PN: You seem almost to have phased out the use of mixed metres as well: why is this?

SD: Modern music has often done itself disservice with over-complexity of time signature and incessant change. The simpler the notational method the better. Constant change tends to result in constant choppiness in performance; OK if that's the purpose, but it's really never my purpose. Therefore I've a preference for the basic 3/4, 4/4, 6/8 standard and let the more capricious rhythmic elements fly about, since this is an inducement to continuity. If I can get the music to look simpler than it actually is, I take a pride in it.

Today's Baroque, almost 'vocal' approach to playing the harpsichord contrasts strongly with the generic pianistic approach of the early 20th-century school of harpsichord playing, but although piano technique is not desirable for early repertoire, the 20th-century repertoire is a different context. Some modern harpsichord works will sound basically the same regardless of the source of technique used to play them, but there are instances in Dodgson's works where real harpsichord sensibilities in the performer can be important. For example, Invention Set 3, No. 1 (Example 5) is a very expressive piece, improvisatory in feel, and it could be seen in the light of the unmeasured prelude. It is marked 'largamente e liberamente' and 'sempre sostenuto'. This can be expressed on the harpsichord by overholding the notes of the broken chords and by 'arpeggiating' between voices. For example, to play the E and the C in bar 1 fractionally broken is an example of harpsichord technique that gives a more expressive and resonant result, as well as a rhythmic emphasis by bringing out the duple time. The use of harpsichord articulations brings out phrasing and pulse, and this can be said for much of Dodgson's music where the voices are exposed, slow and melodic, and where harmonic and rhythmic emphasis are important.

Example 5: Invention Set 3, No. 1

PN: In general, how relevant is it that your music is played by a true harpsichordist? Perhaps the issue of technical style is less important when the right musician is playing it, regardless of their keyboard 'persuasion'?

SD: As such, it's not so important; but I'm a bit upset if I find the player isn't as sensitive as I'd like to peculiarities of harpsichord sound. On the other hand, their keyboard persuasion can mean an overweening devotion to one of the tenets of 'performance practice'. I remember begging a continental harpsichordist to play a certain passage in my Aulos Trio [*Aulos Variations*] with the hands together in place of the exaggerated displacement which so appealed to him, after which he was less keen to have my opinions.

PN: The Fantasia movements in Set 5 and in *Sonata-Divisions*, and the unmeasured prelude style, seem to illuminate further the dichotomy between the piano and the harpsichord in your keyboard writing (Example 6: *Sonata-Divisions*).

SD: I've developed an unmeasured style in writing for the piano too – but it's completely different. I love both instruments, but I do not let them meet!

PN: In throwing off the last vestiges of 'piano writing' in your most recent harpsichord works, do you feel a greater sensitivity to the whole harpsichord aesthetic?

SD: Yes: it's an important reason why I've gone on writing for it – the search for an elusive ideal – a modern music that is intrinsically harpsichord yet carries resonances of its historic past.

Example 6: Sonata-Divisions, mvt. 9

PN: In writing for harpsichord in ensemble, what are the challenges in balancing the sonorities? For instance, how do you work round the predisposition of the harpsichord's treble register to get lost in ensemble?

SD: I agree that the harpsichord changes its nature in ensemble, and each ensemble situation is unlike the others. In nearly every situation its sustaining power is eclipsed by all the naturally sustaining instruments. To obtain a balance, it is the handling of those instruments which is the clue to success. Avoid the register where the harpsichord is to penetrate clearly; similarly avoid duplicating its busier figurations. Open spacing is always good; single notes rather than chords are better for a held background.

∞

Dodgson demonstrates in his *Arlington Concertante* that harpsichord sound can 'behave' very differently in a concerto context; it has a highly dramatic effect, sometimes of menace – particularly when re-entering with a burst of activity after a long rest. Dodgson projects this quality to compelling effect in his fondness for suspense and dramatic shifts of mood. Ornaments and fast arpeggiated movement are also fantastically effective inside a varied instrumental texture. (Examples 7 and 8.)

PN: With the denser instrumental texture of the concerto, there is a propensity for the harpsichord to lose its rhythmic power. How did you compensate for this, for example in *Arlington Concertante* [written for harpsichord, wind, brass and percussion]: in particular, writing rhythmic stress into the harpsichord part? In what ways did the orchestration allow the harpsichord to cut through the texture, particularly in tutti passages?

SD: *Arlington Concertante* was a challenge indeed, being on the face of it an impossible combination. There had to be an illusion of tutti, achieved by leaving 'holes' in spacing and rhythm for the soloist. The thematic ideas were shaped by this – a case of making a virtue out of a necessity. I must have a perverse streak, because I really enjoy that sort of situation!

PN: What was the difference in your approach to scoring in *Concerto da Camera* [No. 1] in 1963? What were the reasons for its revision in 1979?

SD: *Concerto da Camera* is scored for violas, cellos and double bass only (I was thinking of [Bach's] sixth Brandenburg); their

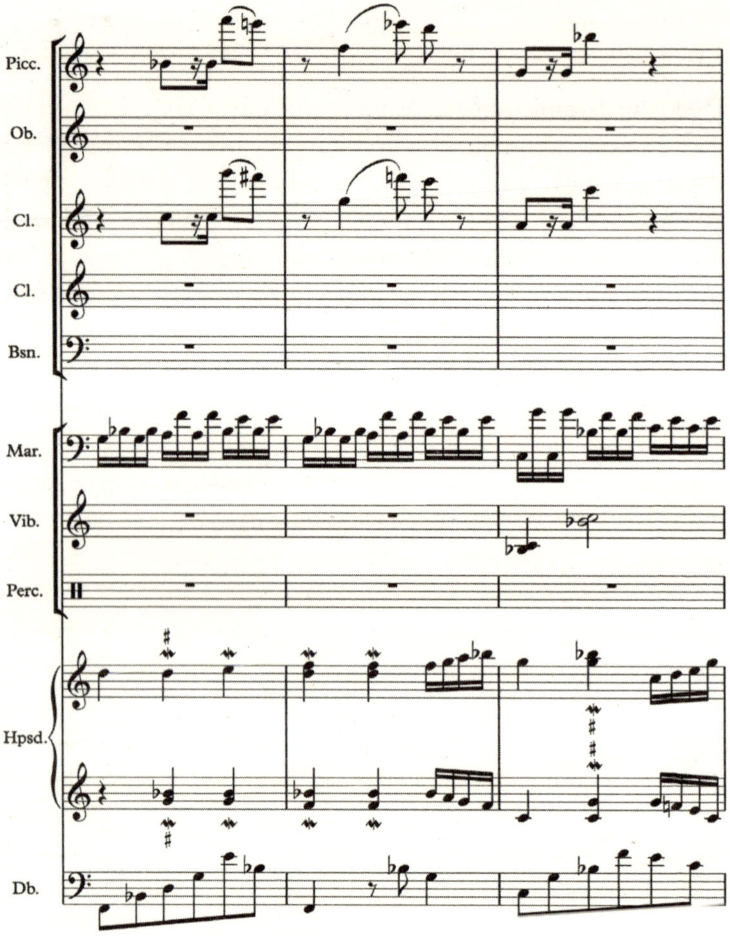

Example 7: *Arlington Concertante*

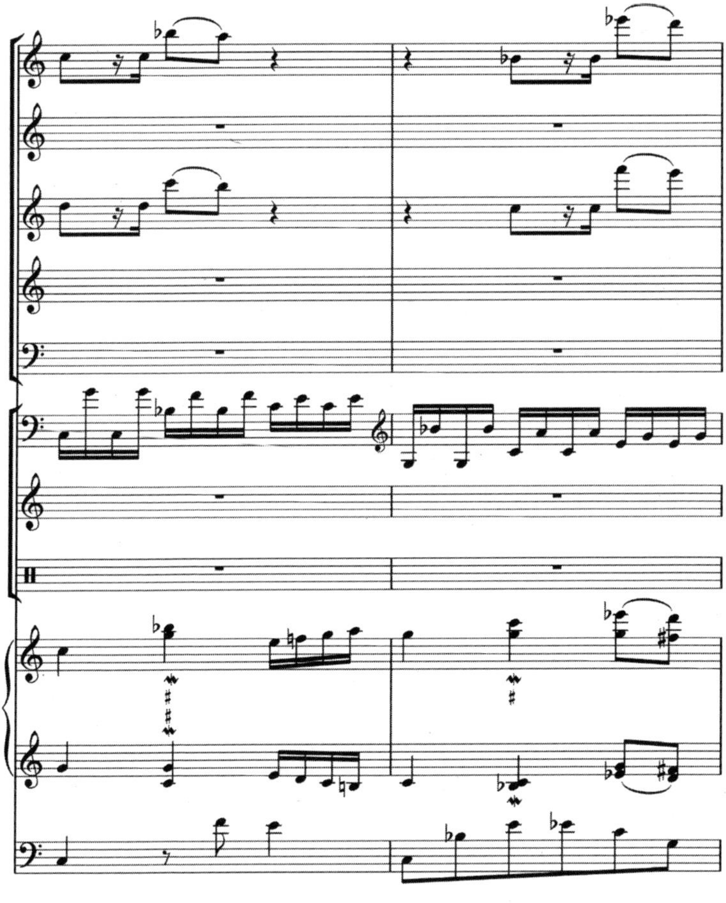

Example 8: *Arlington Concertante*

natural compass is exactly where the harpsichord has its soul. It was a long time before it came to performance [1973], and by 1979 I acted to improve its sonority, its transparency, in ways I knew little of when originally working at it.

∞

Dodgson attended a week-long symposium of his harpsichord music in 1996 run by Southern Methodist University of Dallas. It was led by the organist and harpsichordist Larry Palmer who commissioned Dodgson's *Duo alla Fantasia* for harp and harpsichord in 1981. It featured masterclasses by the composer, and performances of Inventions, Sonata-Divisions and Carillon for two harpsichords.

PN: What was it like to be studied and performed so intensively and by such a diverse group of keyboard players?

SD: It was a new experience for me. I'd never previously thought of all my harpsichord music all at once, and was anxious about a good many of the earlier Inventions. Would they stand up to an intensive week? Would they fail to hold the attention of the participants? They were a very diverse group, in age and attainment. It was not only a true adventure for them, but it felt like one for me too – and I felt I'd been right to pursue harpsichord composition as long as I have.

PN: As a composer, you must have an ideal in your mind of how a piece should come across in performance. Is it more rewarding to collaborate with the performer, for example in a masterclass format, or is hearing what a performer makes of the piece on their own terms equally valuable?

SD: The most rewarding thing is the discovery that a performer has identified with what you've written, and found meaning and excitement in it. It actually adds to the interest if it's not identical with mine.

PN: You have written for many different media, but you show a predilection for non-mainstream 'uncommercial' instruments and ensemble combinations. The *Duo Concertante* for guitar and harpsichord, for example, while demonstrating that this is a fascinating medium, is still a relatively uncharted territory. Few players after Rafael Puyana and John Williams have explored the harpsichord and guitar ensemble, not least because of a dearth of major works like the *Duo Concertante*. Then there are the limitations in distribution and publication, etc.: doesn't it therefore deliver rather a small return on your investment? Or is it more important to you to follow your nose for a particular medium, regardless of its marketability?

SD: Don't forget that the larger part of what I've written for both guitar and harpsichord has been at specific players' request. It's not just my predilection; it's my willingness to be led where the prospect seems interesting. I should probably give more attention to marketability than I do and you are of course right on the general point!

PN: Although there is a segment of the classical audience which still associates the harpsichord with unflattering antiquated recordings, it seems significant that harpsichord aficionados were often converted to the instrument by these early renditions; was it because one was listening without judgement or criterion, and so the spirit of the music came through regardless?

SD: Yes. The 20th-century history of the harpsichord is every way as fascinating as the original hundred years from circa 1660. Those early renditions from the dawn of the revival will never lose their fascination, and are so illuminating as to all that has happened since.

PN: Although the criteria for judging harpsichord performance style has changed dramatically since the dawn of the revival, there are still anomalies in current opinion when it comes to certain performers. Landowska's style, for example, is at odds with today's widely-held maxims of performance practice, and yet there is an almost universal reluctance to evaluate her style objectively.

SD: To evaluate Landowska's style objectively is hard, not just because she was so strong and individual herself, but almost as much because our standpoint is constantly shifting as to what is or is not a 'good style'.

PN: Most people, including yourself, now feel that there is nothing of any value the harpsichord with pedals (such as the Pleyel or the Neupert) can do that the classical harpsichord can't. And whilst it must be said that the tone and responsiveness of the classical instrument bears it little comparison, would we do better not to try to relate these two species at all, and simply to preserve the role of the pedal-supplied harpsichord as it was? The instant registration, and the colourations and combinations therein can add up to 30 or more on some instruments, and there are certain pieces where this can still come into its own. For example, in Elliott Carter's Sonata for Flute, Oboe, Cello and Harpsichord, the treatment of the other instruments' dynamics and phrasing, and indeed the texture and form of the music revolve around the tone colour possibilities of a pedal harpsichord.

SD: The pedal harpsichord is part of history. There has to be a preservation order before we lose them all! I heard a claim the other day that only two Pleyels remain in the UK in anything like working condition. Elliott Carter's Sonata is part of history as much as Ligeti's *Continuum* and Poulenc's *Concert Champêtre*.

PN: Aside from works where range of volume is a condition of the music, could pedal instruments still play a part, do you think, in championing new music?

SD: The classic, reproduction harpsichord *is* the harpsichord of today; I suspect new music itself is out of date if it fails to recognise the march of time.

PN: But are there pieces which could be considered equally viable on both instruments?

SD: The Falla Concerto sounds wonderful on the classical harpsichord; but you learn something about its historical place hearing it on a Pleyel. The application of 'authenticity' doesn't only apply to olden time.

PN: Players like George Malcolm always seemed to be compensating for the fact that the harpsichord wasn't the piano; perhaps his resultant 'hybrid' style is another example of 20th-century 'authenticity', particularly on the Thomas Goff harpsichords, since these were hybrid instruments anyway? Specifically, wasn't Malcolm in fact serving Goff's vision of the perfect harpsichord, along with composers like yourself?

SD: The Malcolm/Goff interdependency was unique. An adequate answer to this question needs a chapter to itself! Goff was undoubtedly ambitious with regard to his instruments being in the forefront of public attention – and they were!

PN: Do you think that the harpsichord still remains relatively obscure to the general public?

SD: I think there's complete public awareness of the harpsichord, but little knowledge of why it sounds the way it does, and only a little more of the reason for its existing today.

PN: How should we raise awareness of the harpsichord in the contemporary music field?

SD: A good first step would be for composers of contemporary music to understand better what the contemporary harpsichord is – to regard it as more than merely a timbre.

PN: You have a strong vantage point from which to view today's harpsichord scene, and to reflect on the changes you have witnessed. Do you feel there is a certain directness and simplicity lacking in some of today's harpsichord playing: that the currently received ideas under the banner of performance practice have had an intimidating effect on artistic intuition?

SD: Yes. The currently received ideas on performance practice seem to me largely outmoded. They were too academic in formulation to withstand the onrush of musical curiosity.

PN: There has also resulted a sort of cloning of playing style which appears to be more endemic in the US and in other parts of Europe than in Britain. There seems to be more independence of style and more individuality among British players. It is due partly perhaps to the absence of a 'school' of British harpsichord playing, but is it also that we have a greater sangfroid and directness of character – a 'no-nonsense' objectivity towards music in general?

SD: Yes, I think we are a little more sceptical, more suspicious of dogma. So, there again, you see how British I am!

PN: 20th-century music is not a medium for demonstrating 'performance practice', as the context does not engender the same sorts of freedoms as early music does, and there is no assumed historical agenda other than the composer's own. The performer has to be open to this and technically versatile; in your own harpsichord music, there is a need for great clarity and technical precision and little margin for liberties within the style. Is this part of the question of why contemporary music is ignored by harpsichordists?

SD: Perhaps so. If I take your question aright, the 'performance practitioner' finds his interpretative role diminished by the exact requirements of a contemporary score, and so retreats to his beloved old masters, who (he believes) give him this freedom. Something in the argument, but a bit simplistic I think.

PN: Do you see it as being rooted politically in the old factions that formed in the harpsichord world: those who endorsed contemporary harpsichord music were 'politically incorrect' because their wider musical concern was seen to detract from the cause?

SD: Rather more in this argument. Dabbling in contemporary music is avoided by some players (but only some!) as a dilution of their application to the old masters – that their seriousness as 'specialists' is undermined thereby. The low-pitch factor plus meantone tuning also play their part in creating a chasm between old and modern music. A composer may want to write for the harpsichord in ensemble, but may not want the partnering instruments to be Baroque.

PN: Has this chasm affected the harpsichord's credibility as a contemporary instrument in your view?

SD: Not too much, for I'm convinced that the contemporary composition that shows strong and idiomatic insight into the harpsichord and its players as they actually are won't need to struggle for its champions. As to the public, that may take a bit longer.

Source: Pamela Nash, 'An Interview with Stephen Dodgson', *The Diapason*, Vol. 92, Iss. 10 (Oct 2001), pp. 15–19

5. The Operas: Two Worlds Apart

PHILLIP COOKE

Try to guess the opera that I am describing. It shouldn't be too hard if you have even a passing interest in 20th-century British music or the operatic repertoire. In fact, you may well hazard a guess at this opera from the very first piece of information I give you. It is set in early 19th-century Suffolk, has a prominent watery backdrop, there are accusations of wrong-doing, madness, regret and the destiny of the protagonist (who gives their name to the opera) is ultimately in the hands of others who may want to enact their own justice on our central character. I'm guessing there is only one work that is springing to mind: Benjamin Britten's 1945 masterpiece *Peter Grimes*, with its dark evocation of an East Anglian outsider and a vengeful community seeking retribution. However, I am in fact describing a *different* opera, one that found equal inspiration in the fertile stories and myths of Suffolk much later in the century, but one that ultimately lingers in the mind just as long as the work that launched Britten's operatic career: Stephen Dodgson's *Margaret Catchpole: Two Worlds Apart.*

Of course, like the composer, *Margaret Catchpole* is not a household name, in fact even opera aficionados may well draw a blank when presented with this dramatic tale of the eponymous heroine and her colourful life. But the tale of Catchpole is one that transcends Dodgson's 1979 opera: it is part of Suffolk folklore and has relevance as much to the banks of the River Orwell as to the nascent colonies of New South Wales and the beginnings of a colonial history in Australia. In fact, as well as the opera, there are various stage plays, novels, silent films and even a musical about Catchpole and her exploits. To cement her importance to the area one need look no further than the public house that bears her name in Ipswich, as far as I'm aware an honour that has yet to be given to the anti-hero of Britten's most enduring operatic work. It is no surprise that Dodgson would turn to this tale for his largest and most ambitious piece and that it would elicit from him some of his most dramatic and memorable music.

Stephen Dodgson wrote three theatrical works for adult voices during his long career: *Cadilly*, *Margaret Catchpole* and *Nancy the Waterman*. (These sit alongside four operas for children's voices, *The Old Master*, *Threadneedle Street*, *Strong Drink* and *The Miller's Secret*, and an earlier work, *Lammas Fair* for adult soloists and children's chorus.) Of the three, *Margaret Catchpole* is the most substantial and thought-provoking. All three share an East Anglian setting and though from very different periods of his compositional life all feature similar concerns, themes and challenges that I hope to explore in this chapter. *Catchpole* came ten years after his first offering, the one-act farce *Cadilly* (1969), and would be followed nearly 30 years later by another one-act romp, *Nancy the Waterman* from 2007. However, it is *Catchpole* that asks the most questions of the listener and made more demands of the composer, and it is here that this investigation of Dodgson's operas will mainly focus.

Unlike Britten, Dodgson was not a native of Suffolk, though he held a deep affinity for that part of the world for much of his life. His wife Jane Clark hailed from the area, and it would be following his mother's death and father's subsequent marriage to a Suffolk farmer's daughter that the two met in 1958, marrying in 1959. It was Jane who passed on her own copy of Richard Cobbold's *The History of Margaret Catchpole* (first published in 1845, 26 years after Catchpole's death) to her husband, eventually resulting in the opera some 20 years later.[1] Despite being a Londoner for the majority of his life, Dodgson's Suffolk is just as captivating and visceral as Britten's and the lack of regular walks on the Aldeburgh seafront don't appear to have dimmed Dodgson's conjuration of this Georgian scene. The libretto for the opera was written by East Anglian writer and sociologist Ronald Fletcher (1921–92), with regular meetings between the two collaborators taking place at the historic Scole Inn, near Diss in South Norfolk. *Margaret Catchpole* was commissioned by the Brett Valley Society for the Arts and was given three performances in Hadleigh, Suffolk, in June 1979.

To appreciate fully Dodgson's compositional inventiveness and technique in *Margaret Catchpole* and to understand the decisions our heroine makes and the repercussions they have across the two worlds of the opera's subtitle, a brief synopsis of the libretto is required. The drama centres around Margaret's love for the smuggler Will Laud, a general ne'er-do-well who promises much but delivers little, his obvious faults notwithstanding Margaret trusts in his innate goodness and maintains her love for him in the face the affections of the more suitable (but much less dashing) John Barry. Margaret nevertheless refuses to elope with Laud: she does not want to be part of an immoral life of smuggling. Laud's accomplice John Luff therefore persuades Laud to abduct Margaret but a chance encounter

---

1 Jane Dodgson charmingly stated, 'With me, Stephen also adopted Suffolk and my precious edition of *Margaret Catchpole*.' Richard Edgar-Wilson, liner notes to *Margaret Catchpole: Two Worlds Apart*, Naxos CD, 8.660459–61 (2021), p. 5.

Original 1979 *Margaret Catchpole* cast: Katharine Jackson
(Mrs Palmer), Julian Pike (Crusoe), Mark Rowlinson (Luff),
Pat Conti (Mrs Cobbold), Jack Irons (Laud), Ameral Gunson
(Margaret), Richard Suart (Barry), Jonathan Robarts (Judge)

in the marsh mist sees Laud shoot and injure Barry leaving
him to be comforted by the half-crazed fisherman Crusoe (a
Britten character if ever there was one), while Luff and Laud
escape. Later on, a heartbroken Barry decides to emigrate to
Canada. Meanwhile, Laud reforms his ways and joins the
King's Navy but a misunderstanding leads to his being rejected
by Margaret and left angry. Realising her mistake and heartbroken, Margaret is persuaded by a forged letter from the evil
Luff to steal a horse and ride to London to be with Laud.
Margaret is caught and finds herself in the courtroom and sen-
tenced to death, this then being commuted to imprisonment.
Whilst in prison she chances upon Laud again and the two of
them escape to freedom, though are soon captured once more;

Laud is killed and Margaret finds herself back in the court. Another death sentence, another commutation but now a deportation to Australia. Much later, Margaret has found consolation in her work in an orphanage where it turns out John Barry is a local dignitary (he evidentially decided on the Southern Hemisphere rather than Canada), they meet, fall in love and the blissful ending is replete with baby rocking in the cradle, although with a hint of wistfulness as Margaret thinks back to her old far home and the Orwell shore.

Dodgson structures his opera into four acts: a preparatory first, an expositional second, a dramatic third and a dreamlike fourth which acts more like a postlude or epilogue. It is an ambitious, big-boned and somewhat traditional offering, with the necessary interludes and introductions provided by the small orchestra (wind quintet, string quintet and harp) who add to the colourful tableaux throughout. The scope of the opera is enhanced by the vocal resources: there are sixteen named characters with Catchpole an expressive soprano, Laud a desperate tenor and Barry a weary baritone. Dodgson tends to avoid formulaic set pieces, leaving the drama to unfold in a more personal and character-driven way, this leading to much intricate dialogue and narrative, especially in the dense second act. Perhaps the most memorable moments in the opera are when the composer lets more ensemble material ensue, particularly the harvest setting at the end of scene 1 where a rumbustious pastoralism takes over, a splash of technicolour amidst Dodgson's more restrained palette for *Margaret Catchpole*. The same applies to the opening court scene in Act 3, where Dodgson's ability as a manipulator of motivic material comes to the fore as a short fanfare permeates throughout the whole ensemble, colouring this most dramatic moment in the opera so far.

Dodgson's ability as an orchestrator is obvious throughout the opera; this is a busy and intricate score but one where much thought has been given to the instrumental timbres at all times. The woodwind writing is especially idiomatic, with long, sinuous lines for the upper instruments winding their way through the texture, often simultaneously providing harmonic support and another melodic voice, always contributing to the mood the composer is seeking to convey. Despite *Margaret Catchpole* being an opera on a truly ambitious scale (it has a duration of nearly three hours), Dodgson rarely wastes a note: there is an austerity that pervades the music (perhaps another nod to Britten) with the composer's own form of tonality shifting in colour, often from bar to bar. The opening moments of the opera highlight Dodgson's nuanced orchestration, from the percussive and fragmentary tutti material that accompanies Luff and Laud's machinations springs the most fragile and bewitching duet between harp and horn by which Margaret addresses the moon (this is then reprised to devastating effect at the end of the opera). In fact, of all the instruments in the composer's small orchestra, it is the harp that has the most interesting and eventful role: Dodgson rarely uses it in full ensemble material, rather reserving it for more intimate moments, or key transformative sections in which the inner thoughts of characters are brought to the fore. Despite the large cast the vocal writing throughout the opera is somewhat sparse, mainly syllabic and often with natural speech rhythms, melismas being reserved for words of emotional or dramatic importance.

The final act of the opera, which Dodgson entitles 'New World: Australia' is both the most satisfying and problematic of the whole work. Following on from the intense drama of the second courtroom appearance and sentencing in Act 3, and Catchpole's subsequent acceptance of her fate, it is rather jarring to find the action suddenly supplanted to the other side of the world and an ending redolent of Hollywood unfolding for our heroine. The rekindling of the friendship (and then a relationship) between Margaret and John Barry is warming and beautiful, and Dodgson's harmonic language also warms and relaxes to accentuate this antipodean postlude. However, the drama of Act 3 which Dodgson has worked into a thrilling denouement feels somewhat redundant in this bucolic ending. There is no suggestion that the actual Margaret Catchpole ever found happiness such as this, and though there is no obligation for the composer to adhere to historical events, the overly satisfying and rapturous end seems to negate some of the suffering endured by Catchpole earlier in the opera. It is interesting to note that 'Dodgson subsequently rewrote the fourth act'[2] before a second performance at the Wangford Festival in 1989, perhaps suggesting he himself wrestled with quite how to arrive at the ending that would best conclude the opera.

There is much to admire in *Margaret Catchpole* and the work is both dramatic and memorable in equal amounts. Dodgson has a flair for the dramatic and the theatrical and there are moments (especially in the first and third acts) where one is totally captivated by what is unfolding on the stage. The love triangle between Margaret, Laud and Barry is a well-worn operatic device, and allied with the buccaneering, caddish nature of Laud this could have become obvious and hackneyed. However, Dodgson treats these characters (especially Catchpole and Laud) with great sensitivity and depth and, to the end, the listener is always second-guessing Margaret's motives and her next steps: she is one of British 20th-century opera's great unsung heroines.

---

2 Leonora Dawson-Bowling, *Margaret Catchpole: Two Worlds Apart*, accompanying pamphlet to Snape Maltings performance, July 2019, Stephen Dodgson Charitable Trust, 2019, p. 5.

Dodgson was a brave composer to take on a project so similar in mood, atmosphere and location to Britten's *Peter Grimes*: it was always going to be judged by the success of the earlier piece. Dodgson had often stated his admiration for the older composer's work and even attended an early performance of *Peter Grimes* when on leave from the Navy at the end of World War II.[3] There are many moments in the piece where Dodgson strikes off into new territory, free from the influence of *Grimes*, but there are other times where you suspect Dodgson would have liked the orchestral and chorus resources that were available to Britten for his own East Anglian fable. Despite these commonalities, *Margaret Catchpole* is a unique and personal response to a powerful tale by a composer who firmly believed in the story he was telling and how important it was that this story was told.

There are both similarities and differences between *Margaret Catchpole* and Dodgson's earlier foray into the operatic world, his one-act 'dramatic entertainment' for four solo voices and wind quintet, *Cadilly*, which was first performed at the Southbank Centre's Purcell Room in London in 1969. The main differences relate to the scope, size and ambition of the two works, the earlier being smaller in all three, running to roughly 30 minutes in a much more compact and restrained form. The similarities between the two are both obvious and subtle, suggesting that despite its very different tone and mood, *Cadilly* found Dodgson flexing many of the same compositional muscles he would use to great effect a decade later in *Margaret*

---

3 'Many years later, Britten's partner Peter Pears contributed funds to *Margaret Catchpole*'s first performance.' Richard Edgar-Wilson, liner notes to *Margaret Catchpole: Two Worlds Apart*, Naxos CD, 8.660459–61 (2021), p. 6.

Catchpole. The Fenland setting, the time period (now 18th century, rather than on the cusp of the 19th), the pastoral hues and the woodwind colours are all redolent of the later work. Perhaps the biggest similarity is the eponymous heroine (or anti-heroine) Anna-Marie Cadilly, a larger-than-life version of Margaret Catchpole who enjoys the company of men and the financial rewards she reaps from it. Like Catchpole, Cadilly attracts the wrong men, is part of a plot to change her fate and ultimately finds (unlikely) happiness with a more solid and (arguably) dependable man. Throw in another courtroom setting and a little of the ensemble writing from the harvest scene of the later opera and you have a proto-Catchpole in many respects.

The libretto for *Cadilly* was written by David Reynolds and extrapolated from a favourite book of Dodgson's, the *Tales from the Fens* by Walter Henry Barrett (1891–1974) which the composer would return to for his final operatic venture, *Nancy the Waterman*, in 2007. The much-reduced vocal and instrumental resources of *Cadilly* led Dodgson to be far more economic with his musical material in this earlier work, though the composer's inventiveness with woodwind instruments leads to a larger-sounding ensemble than the wind quintet at his disposal. Amidst the slightly clichéd (and dubious) references to a 'willing maid' who was 'not too beautiful for the rich young rascals of the Cambridge colleges' with all the associated hi-jinks and saucy inferences, Dodgson still manages to craft some haunting music of genuine quality. The change of season that accompanies the text 'The fen is held in winter's icy hand' elicits a slow, remote chorale in E minor interspersed with a flute cadenza suggesting the winter wind blowing across the fenland; it is both haunting and chilling and made all the more poignant by the boisterous music that surrounds it.

In many ways, *Cadilly* hasn't aged as well as *Margaret Catchpole*: the bawdy farce with choruses of 'Silly Billy' aligned with a downtrodden harlot and a cross-dressing escapade give it the air of an Ealing Comedy that betrays when the work was conceived. Whereas the story of Margaret Catchpole and her reinvention and redemption in Australia has contemporary overtones, it is hard to view Anna-Marie Cadilly's ultimate fate with what is essentially the Village Idiot as anything other than perplexing and sad. Like *Margaret Catchpole*, there is much to appreciate in *Cadilly* (not least Dodgson's dexterity with the wind quintet), and the fact that the first performance was given with puppets rather than fully staged gives the work a different tone, maybe more akin to seaside entertainment and the long tradition that this represents in British culture.

Stephen Dodgson's last operatic venture is amongst his final crop of works, and certainly one of the most substantial of this late flowering: *Nancy the Waterman*, commissioned and premiered by St Albans Chamber Opera in September 2007. Akin to *Cadilly* it uses WH Barrett's Fenland tales (this time the second collection, *More Tales from the Fens*) as its source, with a libretto by theatre director Blanche McIntyre. Dodgson has referred to this work as a 'sequel' to *Cadilly*, and the East Anglian setting, strong female protagonist and economical performing resources (four singers, violin, horn and piano) all reinforce the idea of the composer returning to previously trodden ground, some 38 years later.[4] Like the earlier work, *Nancy the Waterman* is a light and comedic tale of another woman of disputable virtue, with more cross-dressing, intrigue and redemption by marriage that appear to be

4 Jill Barlow, 'St Albans, Maltings Arts Centre: Stephen Dodgson's "Nancy the Waterman", *Tempo*, Vol. 62 No. 243 (2008), p. 63.

touchstones of the composer's operatic work. Like *Cadilly*, Dodgson utilises his instrumental forces to full effect with the searching woodwind lines of the earlier works now replaced by strident piano writing, idiomatic horn calls and folkish interjections from the violin; it is a fuller sound than its predecessor with the piano colouring the ensemble throughout. To date there is no recording of Dodgson's final opera, and it is to be hoped that the means by which the excellent recordings of *Margaret Catchpole* and *Cadilly* sprang to life will stretch to the composer's final theatrical utterance.

Stephen Dodgson wrote over 250 works in his distinguished career from solo instrumental pieces to substantial orchestral statements, with vocal works of all shapes and sizes playing a large part in his oeuvre. At the apex of his output for voices are these three operas that define the mature composer, all three distinct statements from a composer with an evolving operatic voice possessing a natural instinct for texture, colour and, most importantly, drama. *Margaret Catchpole* remains his most significant contribution and deserves to be placed with the composer's guitar and harpsichord works as his most renowned compositions. Jane Clark Dodgson recalls that the day before her husband died in 2013, he confided in her, 'We must do something about *Margaret Catchpole*'[5]: he would no doubt be thrilled to hear how well-received the 2019 recording of this work has been and how the journey to the mainstream for this *second* Suffolk operatic masterpiece is well and truly under way.

---

5 Leonora Dawson-Bowling, *Margaret Catchpole: Two Worlds Apart*, accompanying pamphlet to Snape Maltings performance, July 2019, Stephen Dodgson Charitable Trust, 2019, p. 7.

6. The Songs:
A Singer's Perspective

STUART O'HARA

Why are Stephen Dodgson's songs not performed more often? Is it the erudition of the musical language warranting more learning time for singers? Perhaps, but one could say the same of any number of composers, Richard Strauss or Janáček for example. Or is it the esoteric instrumentations? But those are a relative minority compared with the songs accompanied by piano or guitar. Some singers may find it difficult to practise and internalise music of this pitch material, then have the process begin from scratch again once rehearsals with the collaborator begins. But the rewards are so great! To quote the soprano Ailish Tynan, who has performed and recorded Dodgson's songs:

I've had to work hard to find Stephen's sound world. It feels totally unique to me. When I felt like I had unlocked the secrets of this sound world, what beauty and joy of singing was revealed to me. The pieces really are so beautiful – a joy to sing. There is a line of text in *The Monk and his Cat* which pretty much encapsulates my relationship with the music of Stephen Dodgson: 'I too rejoice, when I have grasped a problem difficult and dearly loved.' [1]

---

1 Programme note to *Stephen Dodgson: Songs for the Everyman*, livestreamed concert from St Gabriel's, Pimlico, London, 1st February 2021.

The wit, worldliness and sense of irony running through the whole of Dodgson's output is amply demonstrated in his song writing. It is, of course, beyond the remit of this short survey to give an exhaustive account of all the works in this genre. What I hope to do is whet the reader's appetite and wish them well as they seek out the recordings and scores available. By 'song' I mean any piece for solo voice(s), regardless of the accompaniment or form. As such, I've included duets, collections for multiple soloists, solo cantatas, and orchestral songs. I am a singer, and therefore it makes sense to explain a little of what I think appeals in these works.

Some Initial Thoughts

Stephen Dodgson's compositional output can be called extensive by just about every measure. That extent of genre, form, harmonic idiom, and indeed utility, reveals a restless intelligence and sense of invention that did not diminish with age. Indeed, the composer explored complexities, both textural and harmonic, in his later years alongside an increasing sense of breadth and declamation in his text-setting and vocal writing. He composed songs consistently throughout his long career (only briefly between 1956 and 1968 were fewer composed, concurrent with his time broadcasting and composing incidental music for the BBC).

For the singer, perusing the scores for the first time, it is often the delicious and well-chosen texts that have greatest initial appeal. Where else but in 'Turkeys' (*Four Poems of John Clare*, 1961) would you get to sing the words 'nauntling'[2] and

---

2 Indeed, according to the *Oxford English Dictionary* this word's first and only appearance is in Clare's poetry. It means 'towering'.

'chelping'? But there is a lot of intelligence and wisdom in these songs too, which needs time and attention to be teased out and passed on to an audience. Solo songs can demand a great deal of concentration from their singers. Emotional focus and intent are high on the agenda – especially with long stretches where the tonal centre is not clear, or with a pan-diatonic piano part. Ironically, the harmonies of a song such as *Winter Heavens* (1951) may seem superficially sweet to the listener but are, on closer inspection, complex and thus demand a great deal of preparation from the performers in order to sound natural in execution.

In early songs, such as the Gascoyne setting, *Lachrymae* (1948), the metre of 'and heavy are the lengths of time with the slow weight of tears' appears disrupted. Dodgson's points of musical arrival are on *lengths* and *slow*, which may seem to be contrary to the lines' apparent flow toward the words *time* and *tears*. However, it is a slow song, and there is room for the performer to emphasise the poetry's points of arrival at odds with the traditionally strong beats of the (musical) bar. There are also occasional apparent awkwardnesses in the vocal writing, such as phrases that may be just a little too long for the breath, and a rapidly ascending melisma compassing a diminished octave (A-F-A flat) on the final syllable of 'and more immense', terminating in closed consonants on a semiquaver for that final high A flat – demanding for a singer (Example 1).

But, of course, what appears unflattering to one performer is a technical challenge to be relished by another! And these traits are far less prominent in the later songs. Perhaps this later understanding of breath is a by-product of Dodgson having composed so regularly for wind ensembles from the mid-1980s onwards. Then again, in a song such as 'The Fox' (*Four Poems of John Clare*, 1961) the long lines and semiquaver rests in the

Example 1: *Lachrymae*

middle of phrases, which may at first seem awkward turn out to be deliberate and theatrical, depicting the breathless flight of the cunning creature and the fruitless efforts of the shepherd and woodsman to hurl their tools at him.

Spending time reviewing this wide-ranging oeuvre of songs, one realises there is a lot of appeal to singers in the challenges, intellectual and comic, and opportunities for acting on offer. *London Lyrics* (1977), five songs for high voice and guitar, is a perfect example of this. The first song, 'London is a Milder Curse', is an exposition of the dilemma of a country-born man-about-town, with the vocal line (sung by a suitably harried-sounding James Gilchrist on the SOMM recording) swooping from gambling den to theatre, being swindled and faced with vice after vice, bad smells and endless noise; this all against a guitar part which stops and starts of its own accord. The effect will be familiar to anyone who has ever tried to get across London on foot. This bon vivant wants to chuck it all in and return to the calm pleasure of country life – his harrumphing reinforced by full *pesante* and *sforzando* chords in the guitar – only to realise after a little breathing space and a *senza misura* recitative, as he looks over his shoulder at the city he's left behind, that he'll have nowhere to hide from his wife. His conclusion: 'Oh ye Gods! 'Tis ten times worse. London is the milder curse!' The song ends with a brief, soft syncopated coda in the guitar which has the feeling of a raised eyebrow at the audience, while the singer must remain, transmitting the picture of someone unable to have their cake and eat it.

The second song, Wilfred Owen's 'Shadwell Stair', is a small masterpiece of characterful singing. Everything contributes to the air of ghostliness here. The guitar's opening harmonics (a tone created by lightly touching the strings without pressing them to the fingerboard, which stops the string from vibrating to its full length – a not dissimilar principle to falsetto in singing) are marked 'with suppressed tension; steady pace'. That suppression, the rests in the ghost-singer's opening statement, and his low tessitura which prevents a full, rich tone from forming all give the impression of someone who is no longer a living, breathing inhabitant of a body. And that steady pace, possibly made explicit to stop the singer and guitarist truly drifting apart, could well be the march of time – the loose, slow triplets of the vocal line conceal any sense of pulse or progression. The vocal line briefly climbs to ecstatic heights as the ghost uses his remaining power – his sense of poetry – to describe his eyes, 'tumultuous as the gems of moons and lamps in the lapping Thames', before sinking back to his rest, *quasi niente* – almost nothing. For the singer, to maintain the eerie storytelling throughout, and return to the less beautiful tessitura of where the narrator was laid to rest, takes a great deal of discipline and stagecraft. Gilchrist's recording gives a perfect demonstration of this.

Not surprisingly the River Thames runs impassively through the *London Lyrics*: what else would one expect from a composer 'born by the Thames'? The fifth and final song, Cecil Day-Lewis's

Example 2: 'River Music' from *London Lyrics*

'River Music', is underpinned for most of its length by a *perpetuum mobile* of quavers in the guitar, which ceases only when we are shown how 'Changeful the river's tone' is. Despite the urban, sometimes industrial, setting of 'Cranes, dockgates, launches, ferries', there is still a strong pastoral element here, 'in sunshine rippling... muted by fog, by rainstorm plucked'. But just as the quasi-operatic phrases in this song really allow the singer to show off their beauty of line and tone, that beauty is never enough on its own. These are good words to linger on longer than it would take to say them, but the meaning must not get lost. The singer must never abandon the impression that they are addressing the Thames itself – easy enough in the song's first invocations, but harder as the descriptions of the river's music become more rhapsodic.

There are two levels of textual meaning here – the foreground descriptions of the river and its paraphernalia, and the deeper, more poetic implications of its music and its role as a metaphor for how 'Men must forsake their source, wander and die'. It's extremely challenging to present such things to an audience and keep them well balanced, without letting one element obscure another, to say nothing of singing well and remaining in touch with your fellow player who, in music such as this, is putting across their own complexities. But the challenge is irresistible when faced with a score like this, when the composer has executed their part with such a sense of balance and trustingly handed over to the performer.

Dodgson's Choice of Poetry

Stephen Dodgson's choice of poetry for his songs was extremely broad. The song texts from his time as a student at the Royal College of Music and early professional period, while not conservative within the trends of 20th-century English poetry, do nevertheless seem similar to the previous generation in taste, for example Hilaire Belloc, Robert Nichols, Walter de la Mare: the sort of texts set by Peter Warlock, C Armstrong Gibbs and Herbert Howells. Dodgson almost exclusively set English for his vocal works (there are two later works, both from 1982, which set medieval French: *Quatre Rondeaux de Charles d'Orléans* and the *Chanson de Croisade*).

As Dodgson's career progressed, his source texts diversified, yielding settings of popular contemporaries as well as plenty of anonymous or further-flung writers, sometimes in translation. Alongside Ben Jonson (*Slow, Slow, Fresh Fount*, 1946) and Marvell (*The Mower to the Glow-Worms*, 1956) resides Pierre Motteux (*London Lyrics*, 1977); alongside John Clare there is the American Francis Daniel Pastorius (*Epigrams from a Garden*, 1977). Anonymous ballads from the Hebrides (*Turn Ye to Me*, 1950) and Transylvania (the beautiful *A Gypsy Prayer*, 1950) stand out, as do the three sets of *Australian Bush Ballads* (1974, 1998 and 2003), recently recorded in their entirety by baritone Roderick Williams and mezzo-soprano Katie Bray. The named poets of the latter are Banjo Paterson *et al*, the poems all taken from *The Penguin Book of Australian Ballads* (1964), but many are anonymous and date from the turn of the 20th century. Elsewhere, there are Enlightenment poets such as Matthew Prior (*Venus to the Muses*, 2002) and William Congreve (paraphrasing Horace in *Jove's Nod*, 2005). John Gay, librettist of Handel's *Acis and Galatea*, is there too (*The Snail and the Butterfly*, 1990; *Daphne to Apollo*, 1997), a poet not often set to music after his death. Forays into the Middle Ages include the medieval French texts referenced above.

There is also the presence of 20th-century poets popular in literary circles but not often set by composers, such as Louis MacNeice (*The Distances Between*, 1969) and Charles Causley

(*Riley & Co*, 2009). The Causley setting – surely one of Dodgson's most spirited cycles, and a boon to recorder players and guitarists – was composed long after the height of the poet's fame. These choices hint that Dodgson was widely read and more than willing to peruse the bookshelf in search of inspiration.

In a few cycles Dodgson cherry-picks from the work of multiple poets on a given theme, such as *Last of the Leaves* (1975) and the *Three Winter Songs* (1972), along with the aforementioned *London Lyrics*, demonstrating a discriminating sense of taste when it came to verse. The juxtaposition of poems often reveals themes and threads which are not apparent in the poems in isolation. Dodgson's choice of text is so often more than just the spark of inspiration, it is an essential compositional decision.

Sacred texts are mostly limited to non-scriptural meditations, such as Gerard Manley Hopkins's *Heaven-Haven* (1948) and William Blake's *The Lamb* (1949). These often dwell on earthier themes. For example, *The Monk and his Cat* (2004) which sets a translation of the 9th-century Irish *Pangur Bán*. This work, for soprano, recorder and piano, captures beautifully the monk and cat alone in their house having their 'never-ending sport', with the cat's purring and miaowing portrayed in flutter-tonguing for the recorder. The monk is lost in intellectual pursuits, complicated but without any apparent outward effort, mostly leaving the business of busyness to the recorder, and occasionally the piano. It is interesting that Dodgson uses Kuno Meyer's translation of the text, rather than WH Auden's version, used by Samuel Barber in his well-known *Hermit Songs* (1954).

Then there is Rocco from the fourth song of *Riley & Co.* (2009). The canine companion of Balearic ascetic Saint Roche gets to express himself in words, confirming my long-held suspicion that most dogs possess a baritone voice. The accompanying tenor recorder and guitar are independent in their musical material yet are integral with the vocal line: they almost behave as if a Baroque trio sonata. Rocco gives his account of the saint's poverty and plague-stricken existence, his return to health after Rocco's own doggish care of him and his subsequent fame administering miracle cures to the afflicted who turn up outside their home in droves. The music points to the hound's indignance at being shoved aside by pilgrims, but when it comes to his take on it all, all he can really do is bark. You can easily imagine Dodgson's amusement as the ink dried on the closing utterance of this wonderful, mature cycle: *Bow-wow, Bow-wow, Bow-wow!*

Example 3: 'Rocco' from *Riley & Co.*

Another notable foray into what one might call speculative scripture is *The Tower*, for baritone and organ (1980), a work still awaiting recording. The text, by Robert Nichols (1893–1944), is a paraphrase on the last supper and Jesus's agony in the garden. Dodgson's setting is suitably nocturnal, depicting a cloudless night over Jerusalem through harmonic simplicity and clarity of texture. A (distinctly non-canonical) meeting between Judas and Mary Magdalene takes place as the former flees the upper room to instigate his betrayal.

For me, Dodgson's piece resonates with the recitative, 'Am Abend, da es kühle war' from Bach's *St Matthew Passion* that precedes the magnificent bass aria 'Mache dich, mein Herze, rein'. 'Am Abend' takes place after the body of Jesus is handed over by Pilate, but I feel the two are more connected than simply their position within the Passion narrative. In Bach, there is a 'halo' of strings which has accompanied Jesus throughout the work, now scored in a much lower tessitura to depict his burial. In Dodgson's *The Tower* the minimal indications for organ registration suggest a predominance of 8' flutes and use of the choir and swell, which to me conjure a similar sense of the twilight in the instrumental colour. Also, the Bach is kept gently ticking over by constant semiquaver motion, and in Dodgson there's a similar sense of *poco con moto* in a recurring ostinato in the accompaniment – minims moving against each other, one crotchet apart.

The Tower could be said to be closer to a dramatic cantata or *scena*, than a song. The baritone's part is particularly well set, rising and falling in a way which doesn't just depict Judas's angst, but also helps the singer last the course as he conveys Christ, Mary Magdalene, the solemnity of the first eucharist and the dumbstruck disciples; a heavy emotional load borne by baritone (and dedicatee) Mark Rowlinson at its 1982 premiere, accompanied by Stephen Cleobury.

Pastoral Worlds

There is, I believe, a case to be made for Dodgson the pastoral composer. This is based not so much on the musical idiom itself, but on the choice of texts, particularly in the rustic characters, the frequent essence of a given season's weather, and the recurrence of animals and plant life.

One of the best examples of Dodgson's pastoralism is the cycle for bass, string orchestra and clarinet, *Last of the Leaves* (1975) in which four poets each contribute one well-chosen poem per song. All the songs have changes of perspective towards the end which make a dry comment on mortality, ranging from the arrogance of Dobson's rose, whose petals are swept away by the gardener, to the melancholy of Harold Monro's observer of the country dance whose blue-eyed, black-haired beauties will not return his gaze. According to Dodgson, Ernest Rhys's leaf burners are central to the work, equating 'man's mortality with a hillside bonfire of autumn leaves, darkened by marching echoes of the First World War'.[3]

Throughout the four songs, the string orchestra accompaniment depicts the characters' inner flights of mood and self-esteem. Listen for the flurries of leaves as the winds of autumn first kick up in the string orchestra's furious semiquavers. It's a fantastic moment of programmatic music. The whole work is bookended by a theme on the clarinet, full of wistfulness at the first hearing, marked in the score to be played 'as in [the] first song, but now very withdrawn in mood'. Dodgson himself

3 Stephen Dodgson, liner notes to *Stephen Dodgson: Last of the Leaves*, Michael George (bass-baritone), John Bradbury (clarinet), Northern Sinfonia / Ronald Zollman, Biddulph LAW 013 (1994).

said he regarded 'this cantata as a turning point in my quest for expressive directness coupled with economy of means'.[4]

Apart from *Last of the Leaves* there seems to be a predominance of outdoor, seasonal themes with wind instruments. The Francis Daniel Pastorius setting, *Epigrams from a Garden* (1977) for contralto and clarinet choir, is an *echt* Dodgson choice in its subject matter. There is the intersection of man and nature in horticulture, and characters who are quietly defiant – some would say stubborn – about their individuality. When in the final song 'Envoi', the garden's master says 'Let Kings and Princes keep the Earth's wide ball / I would not change my garden with them all', I am reminded of other characters in Dodgson's songwriting oeuvre: Charles d'Orléans's slugabed in *Quatre Rondeaux*, Whalan from the third set of *Bush Ballads* in 'Waitin' a While' or the Pan-like figure of Riley.

The choice of poetry for *Epigrams from a Garden* (1977) is perhaps a little less than conventional. Pastorius, an Enlightenment-era German-American, was one of the latter renaissance men, writing on horti- and apiculture amongst other topics. And his didactic *Epigrams* are a poetical instruction manual aping Ovid's *Ars amatoria*, the latter a 1st-century guide to seduction for the upwardly mobile man-about-Rome. Dodgson's cycle includes 'Rules for Entering my Garden', where the garden's owner firmly advises the visitor they should enjoy the garden wisely and 'freely fill thy nose and eyes with all my garden's growth' but should 'put nothing in thy mouth' and should 'not covet, though thou love it'. Another song, 'Weeds', offers further garden-related advisory philosophy: 'Most weeds whilst young an easy hand can pluck, / but when grown strong men then must pull and tuck / This thus

---

4 Stephen Dodgson, liner notes to *Stephen Dodgson: Last of the Leaves*, Biddulph LAW 013 (1994).

apply friend to thine inward state: / what thoughts should die, with speed eradicate.'

Still more unconventional is that Dodgson scores the piece for contralto and a choir of (at the absolute minimum!) 12 clarinets. As a singer, I confess I have no idea what it would be like to sing among the timbres of a clarinet choir. There are clarinets of various sizes and register required, and Dodgson very sensibly varies the texture, reducing to six players in the second song, 'Weeds'. The vocal part is also explicitly for contralto, the deepest female voice, and it would be fascinating to hear the solution of a composer who clearly relished such a technical challenge.

Another set for female voice and wind instrument is *Three Winter Songs* (1972), for piano, oboe and mezzo-soprano. Like *Last of the Leaves*, Dodgson assembled the texts from multiple poets, in this case finding hibernal themes in George Crabbe, Osbert Sitwell and Hilaire Belloc. The first song is about a flock of ducks. The singer and oboe share very little material, though each has room to explore its material fully, especially the toccata-like runs that depict the ducks in flight at 'Turn, and let all their force apply'. Dodgson's expression markings are very precise here, and one can see amid the heterogenous themes a sort of counterpoint of dynamics as crescendo-diminuendo hairpins bring different points of interest out of the texture in turn.

The expression markings also take on a thematic quality in the second song of the set, Sitwell's 'Winter the Huntsman', which opens with alternating bars of different metres, one in 9/8 'brioso e nervoso', and the other 4/2 'severo e pesante'. There is an underlying tempo relationship here (one bar of 9/8 is equal to one of the four minim beats in 4/2) of a type common among the Renaissance composers, whose music was having a resurgence from the 1960s. In this respect, the set puts me in mind of the influence of that period on Herbert Howells, another composer who was fond of reaching for the Italian dictionary. Dodgson at least riffs on commonly used terms like *brio* and *pesante*, unlike Howells, whose use of *ampio* and *attivitamente* has, in my experience, even given Italian musicians pause for thought. This type of verbal expression marking in 'Winter the Huntsman' does still leave the performer plenty of interpretative room! Generally speaking, fewer instructions make for quicker music-making and thus the opportunity to try out interpretations by playing them, rather than discussing them (vital when rehearsal time is scarce). But Dodgson's expressing the antithesis of these alternating metres is a great 'jumping-off point' for a performer at the early stages of putting a performance together.

Musical Language and Instrumentation

Whereas the previous generation of British musical pastoralism, that of Vaughan Williams and Howells, looked to the recently rediscovered (and reappraised) body of Tudor and Jacobean music for inspiration, Dodgson's songs are not so obviously retrospective. And his musical language is in no way simplistic in comparison with, say, Gerald Finzi's diatonic dissonance and consistent rhythmic thumbprint. To my ears, Dodgson's music has a flavour of modernism, even if it is perhaps audibly divorced from the early 20th-century angst characteristic of the mainland European movement. Dodgson's musical language sometimes possesses a modal and contrapuntal restlessness. Though far from the atonal, in Dodgson's songs the tonal centre of a piece might not be as strong as, say, the desire to paint an ironic or humorous moment with an unresolved, dissonant chord. To the singer, at first sight, this can be intimidating. What key are we in? How do I get my note? How do I fit into this texture? Where do I start?

I would argue that for every instance of Dodgson unfurling a sequence of wide, awkward intervals, of letting fly with a two- or three-part invention, or harmonic tempo at the semiquaver, there will also be a spacious, simpler passage elsewhere not too far away. Diatonic melodies are often present but can be camouflaged by the accompaniment's roving harmony. Consider 'Timothy Winters', the second song in *Riley & Co.* Here, the high baritone part is frequently the one laying down the compound rhythm in dotted quavers, while the guitar and recorder play their own, more ornamented material. That said, there is still a sense of unity between the three performers, especially when the vocal line, which has long breaks between phrases as if to give the listener the chance to digest the impression of this peculiar child, falls into parallel motion with the recorder's interludes like runners in a relay passing the baton.

Sonically speaking, the accompaniments are almost always sympathetic to the singer, especially those with piano or guitar, which are impressively refined and spacious. It seems likely to me that Stephen Dodgson intended to have his songs performed by singers with smaller, 'straighter' voices, perhaps with the more intuitive (as opposed to *bel canto*) technique prevalent among the graduates of British university chapels and cathedral back rows until the 1990s.

The songs' piano parts sometimes seem relatively abstract or prosaic, giving the overall effect of a recitative, without regular rhythmic groupings of twos, threes and fours. It is interesting to note Dodgson's comment (in his interview with Pamela Nash) that:

Modern music has often done itself disservice with over-complexity of time-signature … Constant change tends to result in constant choppiness in performance; OK if that's the purpose, but it's really never my purpose. Therefore I've a preference for the basic 3/4, 4/4, 6/8 standard and let the more capricious rhythmic elements fly about… If I can get the music to look simpler than it actually is, I take a pride in it. [5]

Speaking from the singer's perspective, to hear a composer prioritising clarity is really very heartening. With his statement that 'choppiness… [is] really never my purpose', we can see just how important to the composer a strong lyrical sense is in interpreting these pieces, even the more grotesque or angular ones.

What is consistent across the song-writing output is the illustrative role the piano (or other accompaniment) plays, often illuminating the singer's declamation, either with programmatic depictions or conjuring up the necessary ambience to really drive home the singer's subject matter. This is equally true of the songs where the piano part is very much a traditional accompaniment, keeping time and helping to propel the singer forwards. For example, 'The Gypsy' (one of the four Ezra Pound settings comprising *Tideways*, 1950) is permeated by a rhythmic ostinato which would resemble the gigue of a Bach suite but for its chromaticism. The gentle babbling brook depicted by the flowing quavers in *Inversnaid* conjures up the memory of Schubert. And there is 'Tandaradei' (*Three Songs to Words of TL Beddoes*, 1953) as close to an honest-to-god *Lied* as can be, with an effusive pattern of semiquavers and a nightingale singing. Indeed, the text is Beddoes's translation of a German source by Vogelweide. That nightingale is strongly contrasted with 'The Old Crow of Cairo' from the same set: a sharp, restless setting in which Dodgson spots the black humour in the Loki-type figure of Beddoes's bird

5 Pamela Nash, 'An Interview with Stephen Dodgson', *The Diapason*, Vol. 92, Iss. 10 (Oct 2001), pp. 15-19. Reprinted in this volume, pp. 139–161.

who eats the marrow of kings and dwells in Cleopatra's skull but can't get out of the rain. It is worth noting these songs appeared decades before that of Ted Hughes's avian trickster in his 1970 anthology of poems *Crow*.

A Personal Selection of Songs

To conclude, I want to look at a few examples from Stephen Dodgson's six-decade career in a personal selection. Despite its relative youth, *Slow, Slow, Fresh Fount* (1946) for high voice and piano is a real jewel of a song. In its heritage it is reminiscent of Peter Warlock, a 1920s composer with an eye on the 16th century, but who also looked across the channel (via Bradford, thanks to Delius!) to Reger, Schoenberg, Busoni, Berg and Stravinsky. I find Dodgson's pre-1950s songs are often Warlockian in their brisk harmonic rhythm and gestures. *Slow, Slow, Fresh Fount* is Ben Jonson's riff on Echo's grief at Narcissus's death. He wasted away, so captivated by his reflection that he simply forgot to eat or drink. 'Droope herbs and floweres; Fall griefe in showeres' the tenor implores his garden, the accompaniment having already done so with a slippery chromatic progression downward. This setting has instant appeal: simplicity without tedium, beauty without taking too long over it, and a perpetual sense of descent.

Two connected cycles – and among the high points of Dodgson's mature song output – are the first two sets of Australian *Bush Ballads* (1974 and 1998), both sets for voice and piano. The range of scene-setting, colours and character in these songs almost makes a 'Dodgsonian' manifesto. Set 1 opens with 'The Bushranger', a swashbuckling character who is always one step ahead. The tempo is marked, 'decisive, energetic; but only moderately fast', and Dodgson playfully employs a

Example 4: 'The Bushranger' from *Bush Ballads*, set 1

black - boys hol-lo. When the traps give chase (may the
poco pesante la mano sinistra
f
p legg.
De-vil take his po-wer!) he can ride ten miles in a
quar-ter of an hour
p
cresc.
f

word-painting technique to pleasing and quirky effect: while the accompaniment unfurls roulades of slurred semiquavers (whose next move, like the bushranger's, cannot be guessed at), this is within the relatively steady harmonic progression of the 'only moderately fast' crotchets, and the singer then moves through their own part with the repetitive energy of a patter-song (see Example 4). Reciting one's sung text with a syllable to each semiquaver gives a great effect of 'galloping' speed. Ever the skilful setter of English, Dodgson leaves the longer rhythmic values for 'Where the carbines bark and the blackboys hollo', leaving room for the alliteration and plosive consonants to register and ring out.

The next song in the set, 'Christmas', could not be more different. It is a depiction of the sultry post-prandial inertia of Australian festivities which, to gently remind readers in the northern hemisphere, takes place in the height of summer. Through long, held chords and slowly descending delivery of the text (marked *parlando, liberamente* and the *senza misura*), the song is remarkably static. Even the theme in the piano interludes circles without going anywhere: over an E pedal is strung a syncopated ostinato of rocking fourths, later transformed into a charming triplet arpeggiation over the bare bones of a chromatically descending progression in the inner voices.

Finally in the set comes Victor Daley's 'Woman at the Washtub'. Here is a song that falls into the category of religious meditation that explores the profundity of faith through the most mundane of settings. The vocal part has the simple freedom of a folksong, such as might be sung while doing chores, with variations from verse to verse like the melismas conjured up by the memory of the time when 'her feet flew in the dance'. The accompaniment gets more profuse as the poem moves from considering the hard-working downtrodden woman and her bygone youth and romances to the 'dread' vision of her washing the bloodstained garments of the dead; it becomes almost a piano fantasy with an obbligato vocal part, double dotting in the left-hand chords echoing the singer's mention of battles and 'the slaughter of judgement day'. Finally, the washerwoman speaks over slow strummed chords containing a dominant pedal ahead of her final utterance: she is Mary, mother of Christ, who 'will share his doom'. It is only the passing mention of opals ('the bubbles that from the soap arise', beautifully highlighted by the first few rich harmonies after eight bars of a slow two-part invention between singer and piano) that place this song in any Australian context. Otherwise, it is quietly, profoundly universal. How often do we as singers get to sing an epithet as gorgeous as an 'an aureole of steam'? What a gift of a song.

Set 2 of *Bush Ballads* also contains wonderful things. The harsh facts of life are on show in the fourth song, 'The Style in Which It's Done'. Some things in life are simple and some are not, and it all-too-often depends on style: Friend Draper steals £10,000 and gets a mere three years in prison, while Devil Dick holds up the mail in a heist and gets 17, so 'one punishment is over when the other's just begun'. Dodgson makes a wry pun on style in the earlier, storytelling part of the song by setting it as a simple hymn tune, only for the vocal part to break out into Neo-Baroque coloratura to deliver the moral. It is interesting to note that this second set of songs is the only one in the three series of *Bush Ballads* to confront the penitentiary nature of Australia's settling by Europeans, here and in the first song 'Meet Me in Botany Bay' where the protagonist bids a fond farewell to his beloved England as he is transported 'for 14 long years and a day ... just for meeting a cove in an alley and stealing his ticker away'.

We then journey via 'Holy Dan' to the irreverent 'Parson and the Prelate' (both songs observing that outward shows of piety may not ultimately serve the protagonist). The fifth song, 'Old Harry', merits special mention. Its eeriness arises from the fact that the antipodean ghost story seems particularly strange to the European sensibility, taking place, as it does, in the shimmering heat of the outback. The piano is more devoted to depicting midday mirages than any rhythmic propulsion and this creates a sense of eternity that is a real compositional *coup*, and a perfect example of the way that the piano and obbligato instruments do as much storytelling and tone-painting as the vocalists in Dodgson's songs.

This chapter is just a glimpse into Dodgson's song writing. It has been hard to leave such works as *Love's Madness* (1970), a 'Cantata setting of five medieval quatrains' for soprano, string trio and harpsichord untouched. The larger instrumental forces show layers of phrasing, dynamic and colour which the piano accompaniments – as inventive and inspired as they are – can only hint at. And then there is the third set of *Bush Ballads* (2003, mezzo-soprano and baritone), where Dodgson so effectively depicts ironies which are not immediately obvious in poems alone. Of course, the complete *Bush Ballads* have been recorded, but there are a great many more songs which exist merely on the page and I can only hope that this exceptional and varied body of song will continue to be explored long beyond the composer's centenary.

7. The Choral Music

DAVID WORDSWORTH

For those of us of a certain age, certainly as far as the present writer is concerned, the name Stephen Dodgson meant BBC Radio 3. Through the 1980s Dodgson's mellifluous tones were part of my introduction to 'classical music', and it was only much later that I realised that this friendly voice was also the voice of an accomplished composer, firstly through (almost inevitably) hearing some of his extensive output of music for guitar, particularly the two concertos, which I remember liking very much. Gratifyingly, in recent years, listeners have, thanks to the advocacy of an increasingly impressive collection of performers and record companies, come to realise the sheer breadth of music that this seemingly modest man produced in his 60 or more years of composing. An impressive catalogue of music not just for guitar, but for harpsichord, piano, chamber ensembles, solo songs, nine orchestral 'Essays', and much more.

One area that, at least at the time of writing, is ripe for exploration, is Dodgson's not extensive, but on the other hand not unimportant, catalogue of choral music. Written over half a century, these works show not only the breadth of Dodgson's reading, but also his willingness to be (something that rather fell out of fashion for a while) a 'jobbing composer' – not afraid to provide music for local amateur choirs, small church choirs and young people. Regardless of how accomplished these groups might or might not be, Dodgson would find a way.

Much of his choral music shows him trying to adapt to the circumstances that he found himself in, whether this is providing a two-part setting of *See Amid the Winter's Snow* (the second voice part being optional, as is the accompanying piano) or writing a sparkling and jubilant setting of Andrew Marvell's famous poem *Music's Empire* (1972), for unison children's choir and organ, with a second part provided just in case the choir was brave enough! Alternatively, he was not afraid to stretch his singers, as can be seen in his most impressive and challenging choral works, such as *The Innocents* (1975), a striking cycle of three motets for SATB choir with soloists and multiple divisions, which is worthy of attention by any ambitious chamber choir, or *Illuminare Jerusalem* (1972), for male voice choir or six solo male voices (originally written for and recorded by the King's Singers). As Dodgson disarmingly admitted in an interview late in life, 'If I can get the music to look simpler than it actually is, I take a pride in it.'[1] Largely unaffected by the more progressive musical trends of the 20th century, Dodgson's often stated aim was to achieve clarity and provide something that he hoped would be rewarding and stimulating to sing or play. One would be fairly hard pressed to find much suggestion of English pastoralism in his music, albeit some of the texts are rustic in nature; it is rather, as the critic Guy Rickards has concluded, 'cosmopolitan rather than overtly British'.[2] Rickards also points to Janáček as a particular influence, and this can certainly be heard in sometimes quirky rhythmic interplay in Dodgson's

---

1 Pamela Nash, 'An Interview with Stephen Dodgson', *The Diapason*, Vol. 92, Iss. 10 (Oct 2001), pp. 15-19. Reprinted in this volume, pp. 139–161.

2 Guy Rickards, 'Obituaries: Stephen Dodgson', *Gramophone*, Vol. 91 (June 2013), p. 25.

writing that propels the music forward, and very noticeably in the striking opening of his *Te Deum* (1972), launched by a rather dramatic figure on the timpani.

The challenge for British composers writing music for primarily amateur choirs in the post-Britten age was one that was not successfully negotiated by many. Of the prominent figures born in the 1920s, Malcolm Arnold (1921–2006) – who arguably had the greatest melodic facility of any composers of his generation – consciously or unconsciously avoided the genre. There can't be any doubt that his small number of choral works is the least successful part of his output. The symphonists Robert Simpson (1921–97) and the recently 're-discovered' Ruth Gipps (1921–99) did the same, whilst the large choral works of Peter Racine Fricker (1920–90) and Iain Hamilton (1922–2000) – along with so much music of the 1950s and '60s – have been relegated, rightly or wrongly, to archive performances online and dusty musical histories of the period. Those composers that did find a 'choral voice', such as Kenneth Leighton (1929–88), Anthony Milner (1925–2002) and John Joubert (1927–2019), found their music rather pigeonholed in cathedral cloisters, their larger-scale choral–orchestral utterances suffering from the 'one or two performance' syndrome.

There cannot be any doubt that Dodgson 'thought' instrumentally. His intricate counterpoint was likely the result of his studies with RO Morris (1886–1948), on the face of it a minor figure, but one who paved the way for the revival of interest in early music that so inspired his most famous pupil, Michael Tippett (1905–98). Dodgson's fondness for developing small musical cells, a sometimes brittle, spectral humour and a very English understated passion – 'I think I'm just very English, full stop' as he once admitted – is a musical language perhaps more suited to the four voices of a string quartet than a four-part choir. However, it was Morris who instilled in Dodgson a love of the English composer Thomas Morley (1557–1602), a remarkable figure, whose light, singable, emotionally intense madrigals are amongst the best and most adventurous of their time. It is perhaps not too fanciful to suggest that some of the dancing rhythms in Dodgson's choral works, along with solo voices unexpectedly appearing out of a denser choral texture, are at least partly the result of his fascination with Morley's genius.

The earliest acknowledged choral work in Dodgson's catalogue[3] is on a large scale, *The Soul's Progress* (1953), 'a sequence of four sacred pieces' for soprano and mezzo-soprano soloists, SATB choir, harp, timpani and brass.[4] The work is a setting of texts by three poets who lived in the 1600s, Thomas Campion, Thomas Browne and Francis Quarles, together with a striking setting of *The Pilgrim* by the Suffolk-based poet and clergyman George Crabbe (whose work had inspired Britten's opera *Peter Grimes*, less than a decade before). The large forces are handled with some confidence, and the music is a long way from the 'ceremonially inclined' music that one might associate with this choral–instrumental combination, with very few of the rather predictable 'fanfare-like figures' in evidence. Indeed, the third movement, Dodgson's version of Browne's well-known and much set 'Evening Hymn' ('The night is come like to the day …'), shows particular imagination, restraint and flair in the handling of the two solo voices, accompanied by harp and brass instruments.

---

3 Although there are several small and simple but well-crafted choral pieces that are undated and may pre-date this.
4 First performed in 1957 by Eileen McLoughlin, Nancy Thomas (soloists), BBC Chorus, players from the Royal Philharmonic Orchestra, conducted by Leslie Woodgate.

Thereafter, choral music appears sporadically in Dodgson's list of works. There are pieces for high voices (obviously written for particular groups) that lend themselves to performance by either a children's choir or female choir. On a larger scale are *Four Fables* (1968), setting texts by John Gay, and *Hymn to Harmony* (1962) with a text by William Congreve, accompanied by chamber orchestra and, on a smaller scale, *Bird Songs* (1976) and the exquisite carol 'Dormi Jesu' (1995) for three solo voices or three-part choir. This carol is part of a larger choral cycle for various combinations of voices, *A Christmas Collection* (1995), but is an enchanting and austerely beautiful miniature in its own right.

Dodgson's three largest choral statements come from the mid-1970s. *In Wilde America* (1976), written for Harrow Philharmonic Choir, very practically considers what were perhaps the reduced resources of the commissioners, being scored for SATB chorus, semi-chorus (who also act as soloists), accompanied by flute, oboe, organ and brass quintet. The commissioning line on the score informs us that the work was commissioned for the Jubilee of Queen Elizabeth II in 1977, but then Dodgson makes a rather left of field choice (which must have come as a surprise to the commissioners) and acknowledged the American Bicentenary, setting four poems by little-known New England poets – Samuel Sewall (1652–1730), John Danforth (1660–1730) and Roger Williams (c.1603–83), whose rather wonderful poem Dodgson carefully writes out on the title page[5]:

How busy are the sons of men?
How full their heads and hands?

---

5 Dodgson modifies the spelling to modern English except the spelling of 'wilde' which he retains.

What noise and tumults in our own,

And eke in Pagan lands?

Yet I have found less noise, more peace

In Wilde America ...

One would not expect a composer of Dodgson's background to attempt any kind of pastiche Americana and apart from the odd 'Moody and Sankey' moment, and this is indeed the case. It is unfortunate that this cantata, such an individual idea under the circumstances, should not have had more performances.

Dodgson's *Te Deum: with Exhortations from the Martyrs* (1972) and *Magnificat* (1975) were both written for his friend Denys Darlow (1921–2015), the energetic organist, choral conductor and founder of two significant festivals, the London Handel Festival and the Tilford Bach Festival in Surrey. Both festivals, still going strong, aimed in Darlow's words, 'to perform the music of Bach and his contemporaries, predecessors and successors, in a style and manner most consistent with the demands of the period'. Darlow is now a rather forgotten figure as far as the early music revival is concerned, but one who is viewed by many as an unsung hero of the movement. Alongside performances of the oratorios and cantatas of Bach, Handel and others, Darlow set about encouraging and commissioning contemporary composers to provide works that matched the vocal and instrumental resources he had available on his platforms, being particularly supportive of his friends and colleagues at the Royal College of Music, where he taught. Edmund Rubbra (1901–86), Bernard Stevens (1916–83), Adrian Cruft (1921–87), Bryan Kelly (b.1934), all provided sometimes quite substantial new works, along with composers of the then younger generation, such as Geoffrey Burgon (1941–2010) and Christopher Brown (b.1943). Sadly, few of these works have remained in the choral repertoire, and whilst it would be reasonable to say that they are relatively conservative in idiom, there are those that warrant revival.

One of these is certainly Dodgson's setting of the *Te Deum* (1972)[6], written to commemorate Tilford's 21st birthday and remembered as 'sizzling' and 'very exciting indeed' by singers who took part in the first performance. Setting texts in both Latin and English, this large-scale work of some 35 minutes is one of Dodgson's most ambitious statements, scored for soprano, tenor, baritone soloists, SATB chorus and a sort of Baroque orchestra consisting of flute, three oboes, two bassoons, timpani, strings and organ (in both this work and the succeeding *Magnificat* only the manuals are used, making a chamber organ perfectly adequate).

The *Magnificat* composed three years later in 1975,[7] expands the 'Baroque orchestra' a little and adds to the soprano, alto, tenor and bass soloists and SATB chorus a flute, two oboes (both oboes doubling on oboe d'amore), bassoon, three trumpets, and rather mysteriously one percussionist, who contributes the rather unnerving tam-tam strokes shadowing the final 'Amens'

6 First performed 16th June 1973, Queen Elizabeth Hall, London. Felicity Palmer, Ian Partridge, Christopher Keyte (soloists), Tilford Bach Festival Choir & Orchestra, cond. Denys Darlow.

7 First performed 31st May 1975, Queen Elizabeth Hall, London. Hazel Holt, Margaret Cable, John Elwes, David Thomas (soloists), Tilford Bach Festival Choir & Orchestra, cond. Denys Darlow. The concert was broadcast live on BBC Radio 3. The work was enthusiastically reviewed by Felix Aprahamian:

Mr. Dodgson proves here a more considerable composer than one might have suspected from the charming miniatures which he has often obligingly provided to display the particular talents of some of our finest instrumentalists. From the arresting opening to the marvellously conclusive, resigned Amens, this is a true song of praise, direct in its appeal, with bold homophonic rather than polyphonic writing, and an economy of notes that increases the pungency of every false relation. At fifty, Mr. Dodgson has provided a Magnificat that is, in fact, magnificent.

(*The Sunday Times*, 8th June 1975)

of the chorus in the closing bars of the work. Both works should be the subject of further investigation by adventurous choirs, not least because their relatively modest instrumentation matches a good deal of existing and popular repertoire.

Settings of religious texts do not appear so often in Dodgson's output, though in addition to the two larger works mentioned above, there are two settings of the *Magnificat and Nunc Dimittis* – one for soprano solo, SATB choir and organ (1974), and one, in the present writer's opinion, rather more effective for unaccompanied SATB choir (1985), along with brief settings of the *Benedictus* (1969), the *Jubilate* (1981), *Benedicite* (1983) and a rather spikey *Missa Brevis* (1991) written for Holy Trinity, Sloane Street, all obviously intended for less able church choirs, but none on the other hand giving the singers a particularly easy time, compared to so much of the church music of our own time.

There are relatively few choral works from the 2000s, one assumes because the composer wasn't asked (his catalogue of chamber music from this period suggests that he was hardly slowing down). For *Home-Bred Pictures* for SATB choir and harp (2001), Dodgson returns to one of his favourite poets, John Clare, whose invocations of the English countryside and pre-occupations with rural life and the environment were over a hundred years ahead of their time and very close to the heart of the composer. Clare had already been the inspiration behind *Sir John – A Scene from Village Life* (1980), for the unusual combination of SATB choir, violin, horn and piano, and several solo vocal cycles.

Combining a choir with one or two unusual solo instruments, whether by choice or request, seems to have fired Dodgson's imagination. Aside from the aforementioned works there are the *Four Poems of Mary Coleridge* (1987), for an inventive and rare combination of SATB choir and flute, *The Country Wedding* (1987) for TTBB choir and violin, and *The River God* (2004), which

sees the composer setting a text by Stevie Smith, finding solu-
tions late in life to the very tricky combination of SATB choir
and his beloved guitar. Dodgson follows his own frequently
quoted advice, not to 'write too many notes' for the guitar,
which delicately colours and comments on the text, and indeed
seems the ideal companion for this strange, dreamlike poem. All
these slightly unusual choices, as far as an accompanying instrument is concerned, demonstrate a sure command of the technical
capabilities of each instrument, but also a willingness to explore
the still as yet rather unexplored dynamic between these combinations of singers and players.

Alongside his more traditional settings, Dodgson often turned
to the work of contemporary poets. Important figures such as
Stevie Smith (1902–71), Louis MacNeice (1907–63) are perhaps
not so surprising. But the breadth of Dodgson's reading is also

'An inventive and rare combination of SATB choir and flute' –
Four Poems of Mary Coleridge (Barnes Music Festival 2023)

shown in his settings of texts by Hal Summers (1911–2005), in *Lines from Hal Summers – Three Choral Songs* (1997), Ronald Fletcher (1921–92) in *Two Choral Songs* (2005) for unaccompanied SATB choir – again demonstrating the composer's interest in the natural world – and in the splendid set of motets *The Innocents* (1975), mentioned earlier in this essay, a work that sets poems by MacNeice along with Norman Nicholson (1914–87) and Charles Causley (1917–2003).

Composing well into his 80s, Dodgson's final choral work was written in 2008, just five years before his death. *Canticle of the Sun* (2008) takes its title from a poem by another contemporary British poet and translator, John Heath-Stubbs (1918–2006), whose work was influenced by many of the ancient Greek and Persian myths he frequently translated, but also, in the case of *Canticle of the Sun*, by his own devout religious beliefs. The vivid language of the poem, all the more remarkable as the poet started to go blind as a small child and in middle age lost his sight altogether, is brought to life by music that is somewhat stark, yet elegant, fastidious and, most importantly, music that adds something to the text, without resorting to mannerism – a fitting conclusion to a choral output that has still, for the most part, to be discovered. The closing bars of *Canticle of the Sun*, 'Benedicite omnia opera' ('Blessed all the works'), bring us not a bold gesture or dramatic finish (which was most certainly not a Dodgson characteristic) but an uncompromising open fourth marked *'pianissimo'*, quietly questioning all that went before. Surely a fitting epitaph for any composer?

8. Stephen Dodgson's Neo-Classical Language

OLIVER CHANDLER

> The urge of composers throughout the past four centuries to be chromatic in order to intensify expression, particularly of the more melancholy and introspective type, has led to a kind of self-indulgence in expressiveness and inward-lookingness in the artist which I consider a weakness. I feel that intensified expression in itself is a weakness.[1]

—Stephen Dodgson

If 20th-century Western-Art-Music history can be understood, at least in part, as a story of warring factions – of the conflict between Schoenberg and Stravinsky[2] – it seems clear from the above quotation how Dodgson positioned himself within such a tussle. He rejected the post-Wagnerian intensity of the Second Viennese School, finding inspiration rather in the angularity, impersonality and playfulness of Stravinsky. But it wasn't only

---

1 Malcolm Crowthers, 'Composers of Today: Stephen Dodgson', *Performer* (August 1981), pp. 27–30: 29.

2 The most famous example of this historical schema is perhaps Theodor W Adorno, *Philosophy of Modern Music*, trans. Anne G Mitchell and Wesley V Blomster (Continuum, 2007 [1947]).

the Russian pioneer who created the conditions for Dodgson's own language to emerge; the music of Janáček, Debussy, Ravel, Poulenc, Bartók, Hindemith, Shostakovich and even Dallapiccolla loomed equally large on his creative horizon.[3] Many of these names frequently appear in the 'favourite-composers' lists of many present-day undergraduates too. And yet this music is often prohibitively difficult to talk about, at least analytically. Traditional, Roman-Numeral-based theories have little to say about what makes such music special, and those methods that *have* been developed are inevitably somewhat recherché, tucked away among the pages of specialised music-theory journals. In this chapter, I will attempt both to simplify and to argue for the usefulness of some of these methods (particularly scale theory): they are vital for the elucidation of Dodgson's music, both in terms of its construction and its effects.

In what follows, I analyse two solo pieces that arguably capture Dodgson's compositional approach *in nuce*: namely, the first of Dodgson's Studies for Guitar, Book 1 (1965) and the Piano Sonata No. 1 (1959). The former, albeit short, piece is analysed *in toto*, whereas the primary theme of the Piano Sonata's first movement is my focus in the latter analysis.

Much of what I will have to say concerns tonality. As Dodgson himself said:

> Everything I write is strongly tonal. But it is difficult to say, except at certain points, precisely what the tonality is. ... On the whole there is a conflict of one, two, sometimes three tonalities which very often arise from a major-minor mixture ...When I have been

---

3 On Dodgson's influences, see John Mackenzie, 'The Guitar Works of Stephen Dodgson' (PhD diss., The University of Leeds School of Music: February 2006), pp. 19–21.

theoretical about it, I have found the type of scalar patterns which I [have] used tend to have more relationship to the *modes* than they do the key system.[4]

Modes, and the relationships between them, might be thought about in the following three ways. (The second- and third-ordered points are particularly relevant for understanding Dodgson's music.)

1) Modes have the same note content as standard scales (major, natural minor, harmonic minor, melodic minor, etc.), but they are produced by playing up or down said scales from any degree other than the traditional root. If you play the C major white notes of the piano from D to D, for example, you'll have D Dorian. This is the second mode of C major.

2) One can conceptualise a mode as an alteration of a more basic scale, with note changes having an effect on that scale's overall *flavour profile*. For example, if one sharpens the sixth degree of the natural minor scale, you'll produce a Dorian scale. Consequently, one might conceptualise D Dorian as a brighter-than-normal variant of D natural minor. Dodgson loved to play around with such inflections, sometimes creating modes that were both brighter *and* darker than their 'parent'.

3) Modes are related if one can move between them by means of adjusting only a small number of notes. A movement from C major to G major, for example – a standard motion from 'tonic' to 'dominant' – only requires one semitonal change (F moves to F♯). But many other, stranger modal relationships

4 Ulf Müller, 'An Interview with Stephen Dodgson' (unpublished, November 1982), p. 94, my emphasis.

– of which Dodgson was particularly fond – are possible using the same principle of 'smooth voice leading'. Thus, unusual strings of modes might still coalesce to produce meaningful musical trajectories.

Dodgson's tonal/modal approach gives his music a strong sense of *narrative*. While he may have found the idea of self-indulgent expression distasteful, there is always a dramatic thread for the listener to follow. But this drama emerges, as Dodgson would have been at pains to argue, from the music itself. Indeed, as one programme note in the 1970s put it, '[Dodgson] uses neither symbolism nor vague interior meaning – only the music itself, and as directly as possible.'[5]

Studies for Guitar, Book 1, Prelude (1965)

When the guitar began to emerge, in the middle of the 20th century, as a legitimate concert instrument, interest in guitar pedagogy naturally increased. One of the principal motors behind the latter trend was Hector Quine. By 1966 he had become the inaugural Professor of Guitar at three of the main London conservatoires: namely, Trinity College of Music, the Royal Academy of Music and the Guildhall School of Music and Drama. Quine believed that classical studies – the only things available to guitarists at that time – 'were a restrictive influence because they channelled the guitarist into an attractive rut, and therefore blinkered the player to what might lie outside it'.[6] It was not just a matter of technique, then, but also of musical

---

5 Programme note (likely written by the composer), Redcliffe Concerts of British Music, Queen Elizabeth Hall, London, 19th March 1973.

6 John Mackenzie, 'The Guitar Works of Stephen Dodgson' (PhD diss., The University of Leeds School of Music, February 2006), p. 81.

understanding. Student guitarists needed to encounter the 20th-century innovations in grammar and syntax that were occupying professionals, albeit without a 'herculean effort to produce the notes'.[7] Otherwise, an impossibly large gulf would open up between guitarists and other musicians. Quine saw Dodgson as the ideal composer to help to bridge this gap, largely because of his innocence of the guitar's repertory and history. The first fruit of this collaboration was Studies for Guitar, Book 1; the opening Prelude, analysed here, was intended as 'an introduction to the new way of thinking to which the player would have to adjust, as the subsequent studies were encountered'.[8]

The musical idiom is essentially Neo-Classical. Beginning with what seems like a simple I^{56}_{34} (tonic embellished by neighbour notes) prolongation – a nigh-on ubiquitous move in Classical repertory – listeners are alerted from the off that all is not as it seems (see Example 1, bar 1). Due to the way in which the figure is voiced and articulated, there is an unusual piquancy to the A/Bb clash between the fourth and fifth quavers of the bar. In bar 2, a dominant-seventh chord is tonicised by its own leading-tone diminished-seventh; but we resolve from here *not* to the tonic, but rather to an unusual splash of modal colour: G Mixolydian b6. From a functional perspective, this would be the dominant of the dominant. Classical cadential syntax has been inverted: a chain of fifths moves *in the wrong direction*.

---

7 John W Duarte, preface to Ten Simple Preludes by Reginald Smith Brindle (Universal Edition, 1979), p. iii.

8 John Mackenzie, 'The Guitar Music of Stephen Dodgson' (PhD diss., The University of Leeds School of Music, February 2006), p. 81.

Example 1: Studies for Guitar, Book 1, Prelude

The opening idea's thematic construction is markedly unusual, too. Generally, Classical themes often begin by stating a couple of melodic ideas (usually four bars in total), breaking them apart and then driving towards a cadence. Here, however, we have only a single bar of an idea, followed by a reversed cadential motion (bars 2–4) before two bars of fragmentation then conclude the theme (bars 5–6). (Note how the C,Db,C,Bb,B♮ 'chromatic cluster' motif in bar 5 relates to the opening A,Bb,B♮,C progression composed out in the 'soprano' line of bars 1–2 (see the two highest quavers in each). Melodies that fill out the interval of a minor third chromatically in this way are described as instances of motif x.) While the constituent elements of a Classical theme might be in evidence, Dodgson's syntax is subtly bewildering: everything appears to be in the 'wrong' place.

When this opening theme is restated, the initial one-bar idea is more lucidly developed, but the harmonies encountered in bars 8 and 10 defy meaningful Roman-Numeral ascription: ♯II7b9 (sharpened major supertonic seventh with a flattened ninth) is one such (stretched) possibility! Note also that the melodic goal of the appoggiatura figure in bar 8, <C,B>, does not resolve harmonic tension, but rather increases it, placing emphasis on G♯'s 'sharpened ninth'. Perhaps because of the voicing, this chord does not sound much like an extended dominant at all, at least to my ear; I feel more comfortable thinking of it as an incredibly rich 'all-interval' sonority: it contains every possible interval – semitone, tone, minor third, major third, perfect fourth and tritone – between its four pitches!

A chromatic ascent in the bassline, another (slightly extended) version of the x motif, takes us from F to A in bars 7–11. The latter pitch is harmonised by an F♯ minor chord. Because this chord does not thrum with any obvious kind of subdominant-functioning energy, it makes more sense to think of it as a voice-leading distortion of the tonic, rather than as a corrupted Neapolitan: A is held in place while the enclosing fifth – F,C – is shunted up by a semitone. Bars 11–12 seem simply to be transposed in bars 13–15. There is a kind of dark magic about the resultant juxtaposition of F♯ minor with B♭ minor, which possibly recalls the 'Tarnhelm' motif from Wagner's *Ring of the Nibelung*, used to symbolise a helmet that can instantly change the appearance of its wearer. In bars 15–16, this major-third-relation is developed, its occurring now between *scales* rather than *chords*: F Aeolian and A Aeolian are juxtaposed, the latter sounding both bolder and more resonant because of its broadly quartal and open-string character. (The earlier semitonal jolt, from F major to F♯, is thus corrected, but only at the loss of F's major-ness.)

Bars 21–3 expand on this conflict between 'open' and 'crunchy' chords. The arpeggiated CmM7 (C minor triad with a major seventh) in bar 21, played with a barré – the guitarist has to stop all of the strings at once with their first finger – opens out to a more spacious (and more easily playable) E,A,D sonority in bar 22. Almost as if in recognition of the fact that this chord is transposed upwards by a semitone in the second half of the bar – a *horizontal* move to F,B♭,E♭ – *vertical* semitones infiltrate the next three triads, each of which can be described as a root plus or minus a semitone and a major third: {G,A♭,B}, {D♭,C,A}, {B♭,C♭,D}. The diatonic bassline, E,F,G,A,B♭,C, in bars 22–23, however, serves to hold everything together, and the contrary motion produced between bass and 'alto' serves to create a quasi-cadential drive toward the cadence. But the music overshoots the tonic, F major, in bar 24, carrying on to G major: a reference back to the subverted cadence in bars 2–3.

In an attempt to 'make things right', the final system brings us back to a prolonged dominant in anticipation of the final cadence. The first, third and fourth chords of this closing progression manifest a simple vi-V-I (submediant chord, then dominant, then tonic) motion, but the second chord – G♯ minor – throws a spanner in the works. Considered contrapuntally, what is most important is the contrary motion A,D→G♯,D♯→G,E→F,F open-wedge-shaped progression, formed between soprano and alto. Harmony-wise, though, this progression is far more resistant to straightforward understanding. G♯ minor relates tritonally to the D-minor chord that precedes it (an intentionally inscrutable relationship) and it functions as ♭vi (flattened minor submediant) of the following C major. Taken together, the latter chords exhaust a full hexatonic scale {B,C,D♯,E,G,G♯} – note the alternation of semitones and minor thirds, which gives this six-note scale its special character[9] – while sharing no pitch classes in common with each other. They also contain each other's 'tendency tones': namely a flattened sixth and sharpened seventh. For this reason, they can both technically 'resolve' to one another, and so it is difficult to tell which is consonant and which is dissonant.[10] Given that much of this Prelude has been 'about' challenging the innocent F-major tonic of the opening, the uncertain colouring of the dominant C major – Does the G♯ minor triad resolve to it, or is C major a disruption of G♯ minor? – gives the piece's final chord a delicately provisional character.

In 29 short bars, Dodgson introduces the young guitarist to a new world of harmonic and melodic possibilities, while still maintaining contact with the classical structures with which they would have likely been more familiar. Even though it is a

---

9 One can also form this scale by laying two augmented triads whose roots are a semitone apart on top of one another.

10 Richard Cohn, *Audacious Euphony: Chromaticism and the Triad's Second Nature* (Oxford University Press, 2012), p. 30.

didactic work, it displays clear hallmarks of his wider compositional style, particularly his use of striking modal colours to replace outworn harmonies. If one wants to understand Dodgson, there are worse places to start.

Motivic Development in Piano Sonata No. 1 (1959)

In this second analytical vignette, I look to show how the development of motifs – most characteristic of Haydn's, Beethoven's and Brahms's music – finds a new home in Dodgson's extended-modal sound world. The analysis focuses on the primary-theme group of Dodgson's Piano Sonata No. 1 in F, the opening gesture of which (bars 1–4) is suggestive of a fanfare heard from a distance (see Example 2). Characterised by a striking bareness – a result of the open voicing – this gesture enters into subtle tension with the bite of a Phrygian second, Gb-F (bar 1, beat 4). Despite the extended sonority that is prolonged throughout the first four bars (namely, F minor seventh) the counterpoint is relatively conventional: a double-neighbour, F,Gb,Eb,F, figure is traced by the 'alto' voice (the lower notes in the right hand), supported by further neighbours in the outer voices. The 'ricochet' C-octaves in bars 3–4 are seemingly intensified in bars 5–6; it is as if demure echo has preceded the sound that generates it. Complementing this spike in textural and dynamic intensity, the arpeggiation of Ab major in the right hand of bar 6 – a triadic subset of F minor seventh – acquires a semitonal shadow in the left (Eb→Ab→Eb, etc. in the right playing directly against E→A→E, etc. in the left), annulling any sense of relative-major-warmth. Dodgson thus arguably develops the Phrygian $\widehat{1}$-b$\widehat{2}$ 'sound' of the opening through a further, more intense semitonal clash. Modality gives way to plangent chromaticism in the process; a typically Beethovenian form of

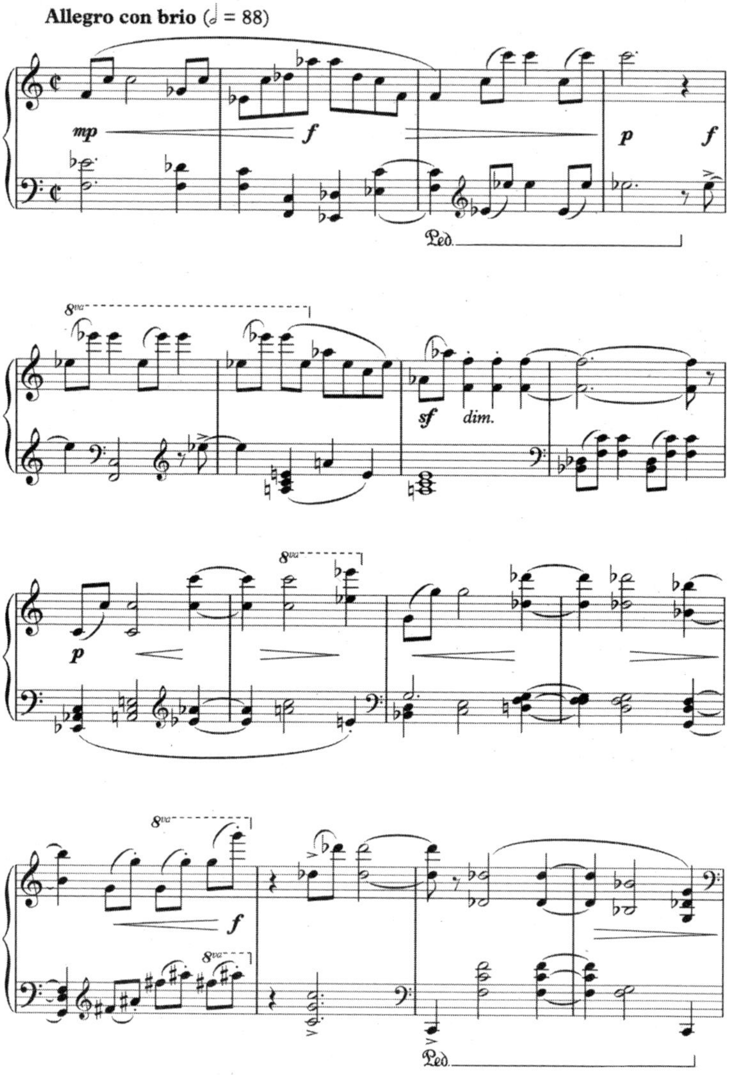

Example 2: Piano Sonata No. 1, bars 1–15

motivic development constitutes simultaneously a subtle move
away from the opening tonality.

Bar 7 is especially striking in this regard: an A-minor triad in
the left hand combines with two Ab quavers and three tolling
crotchet Fs in the right. General chromatic saturation gives over
to something more hexatonic-sounding.[11] We are quickly taken
back to something more diatonic, however: a 'muted-brass' Bb
minor ninth chord is intoned in bar 8, refencing the rhythms of
bar 3. One would ordinarily describe this as a subdominant
chord in F Phrygian, but it sounds too consonant after the
preceding music to be a 'destabilisation' of the tonic. Indeed,
one might even understand Bb minor as a sort of 'mirror-image'
of the tonic major here: F-A-C inverts, around F, to F-Db-Bb.

The accumulation of vertical semitones in the harmonies of
bar 6 is now exfoliated: instead, Ab-major and A-minor triads
are articulated, distinctly and alternately, in bars 9–10 (refer
back to Example 2 – the chordal third, C, functions as a common
tone, while the fifth slides semitonally between Ab/Eb and
A/E. On the final beat of bar 10, however, a marked dissonant
seventh is articulated (Eb,E): the ghost of earlier semitonal
shadowing.

Quasi-cadential gestures then ensue as part of an attempt to
shore up the music's tonality (see bars 11–16 in Example 2,
which feature a series of cadences in F; see also bars 17–18 in
Example 3, which arguably attempt a series of cadences in D).
But, more often than not, harmonies cannot escape destabilising
semitonal dissonances: see the D,F,G,Db chord in bar 11, beat 4,
for instance (Example 2). What 'should' function as some kind
of pre-dominant chord in F Phrygian comes to sound more like

---

11 Again, imagine two augmented triads laid on top of one another, built on
roots of Ab and A, and you have a hexatonic scale.

Example 3: Piano Sonata No. 1, bars 17–23

a functionally inert but extremely colourful 'all-interval' sonority; although it does shade back toward a more normative minor-seventh chord by the end of bar 12.

Similarly intense is bar 18, beats 2 to 4, in which three different tonal functions seem to be articulated *simultaneously* (see Example 3): E minor (ii/D i.e. an E-minor supertonic in D major?) is arpeggiated in the right hand, while D augmented (I$^{\#5}$/D i.e. a D augmented tonic chord in D major?) segues into A major (V/D i.e. an A-major dominant in D major?) in the left. This is a typically Neo-Classical gesture: harmonic materials of the past are presented in such a way that they are prevented from functioning traditionally.

In a seeming nod to tradition, minim Gs are struck in bars 19–21, as if referencing the 'dominant of the dominant' as part of a usual sonata-form transition. But these Gs are heard against a held A-major chord from the previous bar, thus creating a dominant-seventh-like sound. The Ab/A semitonal clash from bar 6 is resolved in favour of the latter note here. Though the secondary theme begins in C major (a more 'conventional' tonal area), A dominant seventh is never far away. The logic of a Classical exposition and its action zones are arguably the by-product of a more Dodgsonian model of motivic development.

A Tentative Conclusion

> I think that my conception of tonality belongs much more with the modes than it does with the key system. ... I love Renaissance music and perhaps every English composer has loved the polyphonic music of Byrd and others.[12]

The preceding analyses have gone into bat for a more continental, cosmopolitan view of Dodgson's modality than Dodgson himself argued for. But there *is* something distinctive about his attitude to modality, which set him apart from his peers. It is not, necessarily, his Englishness. Rather, it is something that likely eludes technical analysis, but which sustained listening surely reveals.

---

12 Ulf Müller, 'An Interview with Stephen Dodgson' (unpublished, November 1982), p. 94.

9. Putting It Together: The Last Work

SIMON FERRIS

My path into the hidden garden of Stephen Dodgson's music opened out from that other shaded enclave, the classical guitar world. My guide was my friend, the extraordinary musician and guitarist Jonathan Leathwood. Jonathan and I were undergraduate Music students together at King's College London in the late 1980s and remained close in the years following. His involvement with the Prussia Cove (Penzance) International Guitar Seminar led, in 1994, to his participation in the first recording of *The Selevan Story* (composed in 1992). This remarkable (and entirely *sui generis*) piece was my introduction to Stephen's music.

Serendipitously, that *Selevan Story* project coincided nearly with the release of an all-Dodgson programme on the Biddulph label, an album which included Robert Stallman's performance of the Flute Concerto, a work written for him a few years previously. I liked very much that *Gramophone* magazine, reviewing the Biddulph release, talked perceptively about 'hints of an English Stravinsky' and noted a 'Hindemithian' quality in Stephen's rhythmic language (it came as no surprise later to learn of his fondness for Janáček), and his own booklet notes for the Flute Concerto included a memorably illuminating sentence which said enough about his wholly sympathetic attitude to music for me to copy it down into my commonplace book:

> I have developed a particular fondness for music which outwardly has the manner of a divertimento, but inwardly is quite otherwise.

This, then, is what I came to regard so highly in the music I was meeting at that time: a compositional language rooted in the European 20th-century mainstream, at once brilliantly clear, deliberately understated and disarmingly beautiful, with its own compelling logic, all placed at the service of an astute narrative sense which knows exactly how, and when, to allow the emotional temperature to rise. Alongside a growing admiration for the music, I was aware, from Jonathan's stories (and acutely observed, affectionate impressions) that the composer behind it all had an impish wit, a blithe manner and a practical, congenial and entirely pragmatic approach to musical preparation and performance. Also, that he lived locally to me (in southwest London) with his delightful and brilliant wife, Jane.

So, when thinking a decade or so later about repertoire for performance at a leading girls' school in Kingston upon Thames at which I was then working, the Flute Concerto sprang to mind as a suitable choice. My own enthusiasm apart, the project would provide a way of promoting some neglected British music and create a context for the students to meet and work with an important (and local) composer. We gave a performance of the concerto in Kingston (Jane later told me that it had been the first – Bob Stallman had recorded but not performed the work in public) and I programmed it for performance in the Czech Republic on tour with the Thames Youth Orchestra (TYO) in 2009, a youth music project I had founded in 2005. Stephen was wonderful with the young musicians, warmly supportive and not bothered at all by the occasionally ragged edges in the orchestral playing. His only concern was that the gestures should be understood and communicated as fully as possible. 'Character!' he would call out in rehearsal if a string pizzicato was half-hearted or an accompaniment figure too vague.

That 2009 TYO tour to Prague established some practices, which the orchestra has continued since. One is of taking abroad a programme made up of 20th-century British music; another is of offering a concerto opportunity to a leading player who is touring for a final time before going on to university or conservatoire. For our 2011 trip, which was to be to Croatia, the outstanding instrumentalist was trumpeter Imogen Whitehead (née Hancock), who would be leaving that autumn to begin her studies at the Royal Academy of Music. The previous year, TYO had given the Spanish premiere of Malcolm Arnold's Clarinet Concerto No. 2 and I was keen to programme something similar for Imogen, one of the most brilliant young musicians with whom I had had the pleasure of working. At that time, we could not muster full orchestral resources on tour, so the more obvious solo trumpet repertoire choices (Arutunian, Arnold, etc.) were out of the question. In the autumn of 2010 I hit upon the idea of approaching a composer for a new work, and, from the experience of working on the Flute Concerto, Stephen was the clear choice.

My first contact was with Jane, via email, who suggested that a telephone conversation with Stephen would be the best way to proceed. (Jane, I would discover, was the organisational dynamo in that household.) We spoke a day or so later. From the outset, it was clear that Stephen was very enthusiastic about the project. More surprising was that, in a complete upending of my expectations (but, I would subsequently learn, with entirely typical humility), he set about trying to convince me of *his* credentials.

To this end he spoke at some length about his long association with the National Youth Wind Orchestra, his catalogue of brass music, extensive experience of the brass world and his full understanding (as a once-upon-a time horn player) of the practical realities of playing brass instruments. He also was not remotely interested in discussing a fee. We chatted about Imogen's playing and I described her beauty of sound and lyrical, songful musical instincts; we also agreed that a small-scale work for trumpet and strings of about 10–15 minutes duration would work well. With that it was, 'Leave it with me.'

A couple of weeks later, a large brown envelope dropped on my doorstep. It contained most of the music for the first movement, elegantly drafted in Stephen's careful, neat hand. The orchestral accompaniment was in short score, compressed onto two staves, with the composer's scoring intentions clearly marked. From the first bars, a series of unaccompanied gestures for the trumpet soloist, this was everything I had hoped for, the music bearing all the stylistic hallmarks I admired so much in the Dodgson I knew already. So, in those opening, fragmentary gestures, despite employing many of the typical rhythms and intervals of a fanfare, the concerto's solo voice announces itself in a very non-declamatory manner. Almost immediately, the at-first purposeful line of thought becomes clouded with doubt, the rhythmic confidence ebbs and the tonal direction wanders. When the string ensemble joins, it does so in the 'wrong' key, with a gesture not of support, but of (unheeded) reproof. What follows is an equivocal discourse, the music interrogating its own identity and occupying a marginal space in which the ideas appear as reflected in glass – crystalline, but with something else always dimly sensed behind the surface. It all seemed to me to embody, in a handful of bars, something of the essence of Stephen's compositional aesthetic.

I set about typesetting the score and had a playthrough at the piano with Imogen. Very quickly she got a strong sense of what the score was asking of her, and the music seemed – miraculously, given that Stephen had yet to hear her play – ideally suited to her sound, approach and personality.

There was then an interval of a few weeks before Stephen telephoned again to talk about the rest of the piece. (I learnt later that he had had a spell in hospital and that, coming back to the concerto, was worried about not being able to complete it – his dementia sadly taking its toll.) In that conversation he suggested (and, entirely typically, sought my approval for) what he described as a 'novel solution', which was to repurpose an existing short work from his catalogue as the middle movement and to introduce at this point three solo wind instruments (oboe, clarinet and bassoon) to accompany the trumpet in place of the strings. All the instruments would then join forces for the final movement. The music he was intending to rework was the elegiac *Philip's Repose*, which he had composed for brass quintet in 2000 as a memorial to his old friend Philip Jones, who had died that year. I was happy with the proposal, not least because the Philip Jones connection seemed fitting, but also because the idea of the ensemble growing throughout the piece, the conversation broadening to include new voices as it develops, harmonised well with the collegial TYO ethos.

Accordingly, a short time after that telephone conversation, I made the trip over to Barnes to pick up the materials for the remainder of the work, which included some passages intended for the not-quite-complete first movement. Stephen was apologetic when he handed over the bundle of manuscript sheets. These were sheafed together with large paperclips and, except for a full score of the reworked *Philip's Repose*, were not in any kind of immediately intelligible order. His instruction was, 'I've done what I can with it; over to you now to put it all together.'

That work of 'putting it all together' became an exercise in puzzle solving, and pretty quickly it became evident that not all the pieces were fully there. The first movement now had an ending, and the second was complete, but the third presented quite a challenge. Its structure was mostly clear, but the materials felt more like a series of sketches than an articulated whole, and the scoring indications (now for the larger ensemble with winds) were patchy to non-existent. There was no indication of tempo, nothing in the way of dynamics, phrasing or articulation, and some of the idea-fragments seemed a little out of keeping, stylistically, with each other. One, a jaunty, chromatic bit of theme with a diatonic accompaniment (and something about it of Malcolm Arnold at his most vaudevillian) caused me quite a bit of head-scratching. Now, I am an admirer of Anthony Payne and Deryck Cooke's (very different) respective work on Elgar's 'Third' and Mahler 'Tenth' symphonies, the scores and sources for which I had studied in some detail over the years. Taking a lead from them, I immersed myself in Stephen's orchestral output, and leant heavily on the Flute Concerto as a useful model when making decisions about instrumental texture and balance. I allowed myself, throughout the 'jigsaw-puzzling' (Anthony Payne's phrase), to 'help' the music where necessary, elaborating little bits of 'connective tissue' and borrowing thematic fragments from Stephen's draft to create accompanimental figures, all in the cause of creating a greater sense of purpose and coherence where the raw ideas did not quite achieve this on their own. The result felt satisfactorily truthful to the materials I had been given, and it helped throughout to know that Stephen would get to see what I had done and approve or reject accordingly.

With the music in a viable state, Imogen and I rehearsed it (with piano accompaniment) and arranged a trip to play it for Stephen in the music room in Barnes. I was keen to nail down a lot of the detail – all that vital, missing information about tempo relationships, dynamics, phrasing, etc. – but also felt a little anxious about the work I had done and whether the score I had prepared aligned closely enough with his intentions. I need not have been concerned. Stephen, as ever, was warm, engaging and clearly delighted to be working with as brilliant a young musician as Imogen. All his comments concerned narrative intentions: how the music should move forward with a barely perceptible increase in tempo following the first movement's introductory paragraphs; how the quiet lyricism of the slow movement should be a conversation of four equals; how the last movement derives its character from its rhythm, and how the final gesture from the soloist should, in performance, be as understated, as undemonstrative as possible. Imogen had some questions about phrasing and articulation: in all cases Stephen smiled, shrugged and deferred to her judgement. He said nothing at all to me about the notes themselves, which I took as a quiet, final endorsement of my work on his music.

That summer (2011), we rehearsed the concerto with the orchestra and took it abroad for a first performance in Croatia. The trip was memorable for many non-musical reasons, most deriving from the fact that Croatia was at that time an untested tour destination for UK youth ensembles. Just getting there brought some dramas – it was two years before Croatia joined the EU and there were significant document and customs issues at the Slovenian border – and the agents on the ground were not experienced concert promoters. Our tour manager turned out to be a former president of the Croatian chapter of the Hell's Angels who had operated as a gunrunner during the Croatian

War of Independence, and although it was educationally power-ful to be learning so much about Croatia's culture, its relationship with its neighbours and its recent bloody history, the musical components of the tour were, for the most part, inexpertly managed.

With the information supplied before departure, I had sched-uled the concerto as part of the programme for our first concert on the Istrian peninsula on August 27th, in the hilltop coastal town of Labin, looking out on the Adriatic. This was to be an outdoor event in the town square, the local promoter having promised us a quiet performing space with a good acoustic and a large and attentive audience. The reality was otherwise. The square was open to traffic (some of which passed, on occasion, between the orchestra and the audience), and the few locals and tourists who turned up sat in the outdoor restaurants and bars barely looking up from their drinks as the orchestra performed a somewhat recherché programme of music by Dodgson, Britten, Arnold, Walton and Vaughan Williams. I felt wretched for Imogen, who had put so much work into her preparation, but took some solace in thinking that Stephen, had he been there, would probably have been in equal measure delighted with the performance and amused by its almost comically inauspicious circumstances.

A week later, we gave the concerto its UK premiere as part of a post-tour concert in All Saints Church, Kingston upon Thames, with Stephen and Jane in attendance. This was quite a different affair, with a decent space to perform in, an attentive and sym-pathetic audience, the benefit of the music being now a little more 'played in' and the performers all very aware of what a privilege it was to be bringing the piece to life in the presence of its composer. One additional vignette stands out in my memory of that evening. Stephen sat on the front row, a very short distance from the musicians, chuckling audibly at many moments during our performance of Benjamin Britten's Rossini suite, *Soirées Musicales*. This music, of course, is somewhat tongue-in-cheek, but it was good to be reminded by such an eminent musician that not everything in classical music must necessarily be received with quiet reverence, and that a theme from *William Tell* played on the xylophone, with a follow-up of mock yodelling and comedy-camp castanets is straightforwardly just funny.

Imogen has since gone on to champion the concerto (which poignantly turned out to be Stephen's last work) in her programming, performing it both in the orchestral version and, more often, with piano. She played the middle movement, at Jane's invitation and entirely fittingly, for Stephen's memorial service in St Mary's, Barnes, in 2013, an event at which I reconnected with Jonathan Leathwood, back from Colorado for the occasion. Jonathan, Steve Goss and I spent a happy couple of hours chatting in the pub afterwards about Stephen and his music, reminding me that of all my meetings with remarkable men, my encounter with Stephen Dodgson had been one of the most instructive, musically and personally, and one for which I remain lastingly grateful.

List of Compositions

Date unknown but very likely fairly early compositions:

Mrs Hen (nursery rhyme) for mid-range voice & piano
All Bells in Paradise, a Corpus Christi carol for upper-voice (SSA) choir
Lullaby for upper-voice (SSA) choir
Winter for upper-voice (SSA) choir
Falan-Tiding for unaccompanied two-part choir
See Amid the Winter Snow for two-part upper voices (optional second part & optional piano)

1946 *Five Eyes* for high voice & piano
       Slow, Slow, Fresh Fount for high voice & piano
1947 *Saints and Sinners*, five songs for high voice & piano (withdrawn)
       Inversnaid for high voice & piano
       Nocturne for horn & piano
       The Saltmarsh for soprano, contralto, cor anglais, harp & strings (withdrawn)
       The Chimney Sweep for voice & piano (withdrawn)
1948 *Divertimento* for clarinet & two bassoons
       Fantasy String Quartet
       Heaven-Haven for mid-range voice & piano
       Lachrymae for high voice & piano
       Variations for orchestra (withdrawn)
       Pandora's Box for bass clarinet & piano (withdrawn)

1949 *Three Bagatelles* for piano (withdrawn)
      Prelude and Fugue in C for piano (withdrawn)
      The Lamb for high voice & piano
      Sonata for piano duet
      Suite in E for violin & piano
      Irishry, four songs for high voice & piano
      Rags and Bones (No. 4 of *Irishry*) for high voice & guitar (rev. 1961)
      Two Northumbrian Folsongs, arranged for voice & piano
1950 *Three Dances* for violin & piano
      Three Fragments from the Divan of Hafiz for bass voice &
      orchestra (withdrawn)
      Piano Quartet (withdrawn)
      The Stone for high voice & piano
      Tideways: Four Poems of Ezra Pound for high voice & piano
      A Gypsy Prayer for high voice & piano
      Piano Sonata in C sharp minor (withdrawn)
      Serenade for viola & orchestra (withdrawn)
      Divertimento for flute & string orchestra (withdrawn)
      Taras Bulba, overture for orchestra
      Nightfall, two songs for soprano & piano
      A Bohemian Entertainment for piano duet
      The Sunflower for high voice & piano
      Turn Ye To Me, arrangement of a Hebridean air for mid-range
      voice & piano
1951 Three-part Songs for girls' voices
      String Trio No. 1 in A
      A Dance Overture for chamber orchestra
      Piano Sonata in B major (withdrawn)
      Taming the Piano (Studies for teaching) for piano
      String Quartet in A (withdrawn)
      Winter Heavens for high voice & piano
      Sonatina in D for violin & cello
1952 *Fantasy* for solo harp
      Tournament for Twenty Fingers (Part 1) for two pianos

Symphony in E flat for chamber orchestra

Capriccio and *Finale* for flute, clarinet, harp & string trio

Three Airs from the Western Highlands, arranged for voice & harp

Lammas Fair, operetta in one act for soloists, children's chorus & piano

All This Night Shrill Chanticleer for choir & organ

Prelude, Nocturne and Toccata for guitar

Overture for string orchestra

Sonata in D minor for viola & piano

1953 *The Soul's Progress*, four sacred pieces for soli, choir, harp, timpani & brass

Ceremonial Overture: Rigel for orchestra

Two Hymns for unaccompanied choir

Three Songs (to Words of TL Beddoes) for high voice & piano

String Quartet in B minor

Rondo in A flat for piano

1954 *The Old Master*, opera in three acts for equal voices & piano

Symphony in A flat for chamber orchestra

Intermezzo for orchestra

Ten Variations for violin & piano

Tournament for Twenty Fingers (Part 2) for two pianos

1955 Five Occasional Pieces for guitar

Dale Folk, partsongs for two-part chorus & piano (or four clarinets, arr. 1978)

Allegretto con Grazia for cello & piano

Six Inventions (Set 1) for harpsichord

Cello Concerto

Saints Day for orchestra

1956 *The Mower to the Glow-Worms* for high voice & piano

Serenade for viola & orchestra

Three Russian Pieces (Set 1), arrangements of piano pieces for orchestra

Eight Fanciful Pieces for piano

Threadneedle Street, comic opera in one act, for soli, chorus & piano

Guitar Concerto No. 1 for guitar & chamber orchestra

1957 *Three Russian Pieces* (Set 2), arrangements of piano pieces for
orchestra
Suite in C minor for oboe & piano
Suite for brass septet
Three Light Pieces for orchestra: No. 1 'Sundown' for flute, harp &
strings; Nos. 2 & 3 'Idyll' and 'Pizźicato Holiday' for strings only
Symphony in C for orchestra

1958 *Variations in A flat on an original theme by Schubert* for orchestra
The Dowie Houms O' Yarrow for free-range voice & piano
Duo for flute & harp
Quintet for piano & wind quartet
The Kingdom of Scotland, film score for small orchestra
Seven Miniatures for viola & piano

1959 *Variations on an Air from 'The Bartered Bride'* for four flutes & strings
Piano Concerto for piano & orchestra
Piano Sonata No. 1 (in F)
Nocturne for string orchestra
String Quartet in F minor
Serenade for oboe, clarinet & bassoon
Pastoral Sonata for flute, guitar & cello (rev. 1998)

1960 *Sinfonia Concertante* for wind quintet, brass, timpani, percussion
& strings
On the Menu, film score for small orchestra
Depth Charge, film score
Villanelle for orchestra

1961 Concerto for viola da gamba & chamber orchestra
The Old Cigarette Lighter, entertainment for children, for narrator,
flute, oboe & piano (also arranged for narrator & wind quintet in
1984; another version, entitled *Tinderbox*, for piano & narrator/
pianist-narrator, was made in 1998)
Six Inventions (Set 2) for harpsichord
The Beaux's Stratagem, incidental music for BBC production
Four Poems of John Clare for high voice & guitar

1962   Overture for 'The Mikado' for orchestra (after Arthur Sullivan)
       Five Impromptus for piano (rev. first impromptu in 1985 and
       confined whole set to be Three Impromptus – the first three)
       Gounod: Two Songs, arranged for high voice & guitar
       Two Songs from Love's Labour's Lost for unaccompanied voices
       Hymn to Harmony for upper-voice (SSA) choir with semi-chorus
       & chamber orchestra

1963   Partita No. 1 for guitar
       Concerto da Camera No. 1 for harpsichord & lower strings
       (rev. 1979)
       Strong Drink, opera in three acts for mixed young voices
       (semi-chorus six high solo voices, main chorus SSB) &
       piano duet
       Sonata in A for viola & piano
       Sonatina in B minor for solo violin
       Sonata for brass quintet

1964   *Sinfonietta* for orchestra
       String Trio No. 2
       Psalm 19 for unison voices (or solo voice) & organ
       Love for Love, incidental music for BBC production

1965   20 Studies for guitar (with Hector Quine)
       Concerto da Camera No. 2 for flute, clarinet & string orchestra
       Suite for Wind Quintet
       The Nativity for unison & two-part children's chorus & piano
       (optional organ, flute & percussion)
       Toccata No. 1 in C for organ

1966   *The Old Bachelor*, incidental music for BBC production
       Piano Quintet No. 1
       Toccata No. 2 in D for organ

1967   Suite No. 1 for Clavichord (rev. 2006)
       Sonata for cor anglais & piano
       Carillon for two harpsichords
       Duo for flute & viola
       The Gay Lothario and Mrs Grundy, incidental music for BBC drama

Piano Trio No. 1 ('Methought this other Night'), Diversions on
an Air by Robert Jones

Sonata for horn & piano

1968 *La Veneziana*, incidental music for BBC production, for voice
& ensemble

Sarabande for guitar

Duo Concertante for guitar & harpsichord

Four Fables for upper-voice (SSA) choir & orchestra

Four Moods of the Wind for piano

Cadilly, entertainment for soprano, mezzo-soprano, baritone,
bass & wind quintet

Sonata for cello & piano

1969 Bassoon Concerto for bassoon & chamber orchestra

Suite No. 2 for Clavichord (rev. 2006)

Benedictus for unaccompanied choir

The Boat Race for children's voices, recorders & percussion

The Ghost of a Play, incidental music for BBC production

Concerto da Camera No. 3 for solo violin, two flutes & string
orchestra

Perkin Warbeck, incidental music for BBC production, for ensemble

The Distances Between for soprano, baritone & piano

Fantasy-Divisions for guitar

Ballade for solo harp

1970 *Women In Power*, incidental music for BBC production

Six Inventions (Set 3) for harpsichord

Variazioni Concertanti for flute, oboe, violin, cello & harpsichord

Five Occasional Pieces for cello & piano

Love's Madness for high voice, string trio & harpsichord

Warbeck Dances for recorder & harpsichord (substantially revised
version made in 2002)

Le Morte d'Arthur, incidental music for BBC production, for
soprano & ensemble

Henry VI, incidental music for BBC production, for orchestra of
27 players

Mikis Theodorakis: Seven Songs of Federico Lorca, arranged for voice & guitar

1971 *Macbeth*, incidental music for BBC production, for mixed ensemble
Concerto da Camera No. 4 for piano & string orchestra
The Perilous Stick, a study in conducting, for orchestra
Sir Gawain and the Green Knight, incidental music for BBC drama
Collection of String Pieces (various instruments) for the ABRSM

1972 Guitar Concerto No. 2 for guitar & chamber orchestra
Three Winter Songs for high voice, oboe & piano
Suite in D for oboe & harpsichord
A Journey to London, incidental music for BBC production, for ensemble
The Silent Woman, incidental music for BBC production, for voice & ensemble
Music's Empire, for unison/two-part children's choir & organ
Te Deum for soloists, choir & orchestra
Illuminare Jerusalem for lower-voice (AATBarBarB) vocal consort

1973 *The Miller's Secret*, children's opera in one act, for children's choir & seven-instrument wind & string ensemble
Piano Trio No. 2 in One Movement (Canonic Episodes)
A Bag of Winds for narrator & five string quartets (optional double bass)
Trio for oboe, bassoon & piano
Quintet for guitar & string quartet
Progressive Reading for Guitarists, short exercises for guitar (with Hector Quine)

1974 Wind Symphony for wind orchestra (rev. 1999)
Bush Ballads (1st series) for mid-range voice & piano
Serenade for guitar
Duo for cello & guitar
Concertino for piano & percussion
Magnificat and *Nunc Dimittis* for choir & organ
Before the Paling of the Stars for unaccompanied choir
Fanfare for three trumpets & three trombones

The London Cuckolds, incidental music for BBC radio, for
small orchestra
Solway Suite for flute, viola (or cello) & harp
Erik Satie: Gymnopédie No. 1, arranged for piano & strings
12 Introductory Studies for guitar (with Hector Quine)

1975 *Last of the Leaves* for bass, clarinet & string orchestra
Trio for baryton, viola & cello
Magnificat for soloists, choir & orchestra
Sheba's Trio for two oboes d'amore & bassoon
Shine and Shade for recorder & harpsichord
Piano Sonata No. 2
The Innocents, three motets for unaccompanied SSATBB choir
Septet Variations for flute, clarinet, harp & string quartet
Collection of Wind Pieces (various instruments) for the ABRSM
Scarlatti: Two Sonatas, arranged for brass quintet

1976 *Capriccio* for flute, violin, cello & piano
Dialogues for guitar & harpsichord
The Eagle: Tone Poem after Tennyson for wind orchestra (rev. 2002)
Scarlatti: Six Sonatas, arranged for brass quintet
Gipsy Songs for mezzo-soprano, clarinet & piano
Partita No. 2 for guitar
In Wilde America, cantata for six soloists, choir with semi-chorus,
flute, oboe, organ & brass quintet
Take Two, five short simple but progressive duets for two guitars
Bird Songs for upper-voice (SSA) choir

1977 *Epigrams from a Garden*, song cycle for contralto with clarinet choir
Matelot: Diversions after Grieg's Sailor's Song for wind orchestra
Legend for guitar
Sonata for wind quintet
William Inglot: A Galliard Ground, arranged for four trumpets
(also arr. for brass quintet, 1987)
Interlude (Summer Daydream) for guitar
John Clare's Wooing Songs for countertenor, tenor, baritone & piano
Aulos Variations for flute, oboe & harpsichord

John Munday: *Munday's Joy,* arranged for brass ensemble
Bagatelles for four clarinets
London Lyrics for high voice & guitar
Daphne to Apollo for soprano & baryton

1978 Orlando Gibbons: *The Queen's Command*, arranged for
brass ensemble
Never Trust a Spider, entertainment for narrator, audience &
seven clarinets
Caprice after Puck for solo viola
Fantasia for Six Brass for three trumpets & three trombones
John Bull: *The Spanish Pavan*, arranged for brass ensemble
Merlin for guitar
12 Transitional Studies for guitar (with Hector Quine)

1979 *Margaret Catchpole: Two Worlds Apart,* opera in four acts for
soloists, string quartet, double bass, wind quintet & harp
Concerto da Camera No. 5 for two oboes, two bassoons &
string orchestra
Stanzas, variations in *concertante* style for wind orchestra
Follow the Star, fantasy for three guitars on an old Dutch
Christmas Hymn

1980 *Duetto Scherzando* for flute & clarinet
Capriccio for flute & guitar
Essay No. 1 for orchestra
Ode for harp & string orchestra
The Tower for baritone & organ
Sir John – A Scene from Village Life for choir, violin, horn & piano
Etude-Caprice for guitar
Personent Hodie, fantasy on an ancient carol for large guitar
ensemble

1981 *Canzona* for massed cellos
Duo alla Fantasia for harp & harpsichord
Jubilate for unaccompanied choir
Handel: *The Harmonious Blacksmith*, arranged for brass octet
Four Pieces by Rameau, arranged for brass octet

Essay No. 2 for orchestra

Partita No. 3 for guitar

Three Christmas Pieces, arranged for brass ensemble: Schütz: *Die Weisen aus dem Morgenlande*, for three trombones, horn, tuba & organ; *God Rest Ye Merry Gentlemen*, for four trumpets, four trombones, tuba & drum; *Lord Jesus Hath a Garden*, brass quintet

1982 Sonata for Four for oboe, violin, cello & harpsichord

Sonata-Divisions for solo harpsichord

Madrigal for two trumpets & organ

Quatre Rondeaux de Charles d'Orléans for high voice & harpsichord

Chanson de Croisade for countertenor & harpsichord

Sonata for Three for flute, viola & guitar

Five Occasional Pieces for violin & piano

Antonio Soler: Two Sonatas, arranged for brass quintet

Essay No. 3 for orchestra

1983 *Hymnus de Sancto Stephano* for soprano & guitar ensemble

Sketchbook for two lutes

Clarinet Concerto for clarinet & chamber orchestra

Piano Sonata No. 3 (Variations on a Rhythm)

Benedicite for unaccompanied choir

Divertissement for violin & guitar ensemble

1984 Essay No. 4 for orchestra

Masque for oboe band & bassoons

Dream Sequence, incidental music for oboe, clarinet & string trio

Capriccio Concertante No. 1 for clarinet & symphonic wind orchestra

Orion for clarinet quartet & brass quintet

12 Introductory Studies for guitar (with Hector Quine)

At Sight, 60 graded sight reading tests for guitar (with Hector Quine)

'Tis Almost One', five anthems for choir & organ

Eliza at the Temple for soprano & tenor with flute (or violin), cello & harpsichord

String Quartet No. 1

1985 *Magnificat* and *Nunc Dimittis* for unaccompanied choir

Six Inventions (Set 4) for harpsichord
Partita for solo cello
Concerto for bass trombone & orchestra
Essay No. 5 for orchestra
Music's Duel for soprano, bass & lute

1986   *Songs of the Heart*, four partsongs for unaccompanied choir
      Festive Sequence for piano accordion
      Baermann's Treasure for clarinet & piano
      In Search of Folly for flute & guitar
      String Quintet
      Arlington Concertante for harpsichord, wind, brass, double bass
      & percussion
      Double Take, five duets for guitar duo (with Hector Quine)
      Studies in Duo for guitar duo (with Hector Quine)

1987   *Four Poems of Mary Coleridge* for choir & flute
      The Country Wedding for lower-voice (TTBB) choir & violin
      Sonata for oboe & piano
      Intermezzo (Citharae Chordae pro Pace) for four guitars
      Double Take, five duets for two guitars
      Studies in Duo for two guitars
      Four Pieces, each for a single wind instrument & piano
      String Quartet No. 2

1988   *Stemma* for guitar
      Two Simple Pieces for flute & piano
      The Tease for oboe & piano
      Symphony in One Movement for chamber orchestra
      Promenade I for two guitars
      Promenade II, arr. of *Promenade I* for wind quintet
      Piano Sonata No. 4
      Crossways for brass quintet
      La sablesienne for guitar
      Invocation for unaccompanied choir

1989   *Sinfonia: Troia-Nova* for chamber orchestra
      String Quartet No. 3

The Troubled Midnight for guitar
Three Attic Dances for guitar

1990 Partita No. 4 for guitar
Five Occasional Pieces for flute & piano
Flowers of London Town for symphonic wind orchestra
Marchrider for wind orchestra (rev. 1999)
Duo Concerto for violin, guitar & string orchestra
Cor Leonis for solo horn
Countdown for oboe & harp
The Snail and the Butterfly for two tenors (or high voices) & harpsichord

1991 *Spice of Life* for brass quintet
Essay No. 6 for orchestra
Flute Concerto for flute & string orchestra
Wind Miniatures, each for a single wind instrument & piano
Ten Miniatures for guitar
Missa Brevis for unaccompanied choir
Bandwagon, five occasional pieces for wind orchestra
Triptych for organ
O Swallow! for flute in A or G & piano
Excursions for brass quintet
Ode to the Guitar, ten miniatures (with Hector Quine)

1992 *The Selevan Story* for flute, violin, guitar duo & guitar ensemble
Piano Sonata No. 5
Pastourelle for guitar duo
Essay No. 7 for string orchestra
Luton Variations for piano duet (part of a composite work with four other composers)

1993 *Solitaire* for solo trombone
Six Inventions (Set 5) for harpsichord
String Quartet No. 4
Oboe Quartet for oboe & string trio

1994 *Your Eyes Smile Peace*, sonnet for brass band

Two Pieces for solo alto flute

The Midst of Life for solo guitar

Riversong, rhapsody for two guitars

Piano Sonata No. 6

Fiddler's Country Wedding for violin & piano

Ellen's Waltz for piano

Partita for Ten Wind Instruments for double wind quintet

The Faery Beam Upon You for solo alto flute

The Silver Tube for solo alto flute

1995 Anatoly Lyadov: Eight Russian Folksongs, Op. 58, arranged for wind quintet

A Christmas Collection, partsongs for unaccompanied voices

Divertimento for Four for trumpet, horn, tuba & piano

Baermann – The Sequel for clarinet & piano

The Rising of Job for chamber orchestra

The New Terpsichore, Book 1, for violin & harpsichord

Five Penny Pieces for wind quintet

1996 *Toccata for the New Year* for organ

Change-Ringers for four guitars (rev. 2001)

String Sextet for two violins, two violas & two cellos

Parker's Piece for piano

The New Terpsichore, Book 2, for violin & harpsichord

Divertimento for orchestra

Two Romantic Pieces (Set A) for cello & piano

1997 *Pieces of Eight* for wind octet

Excursions for brass quintet

Daphne to Apollo for soprano & guitar (after 1977 version for soprano & baryton)

Rendezvous for 13 instruments, for wind, brass & double bass

Flood, an entertainment for wind quintet, with narration spoken by the players

The Maze for solo recorder

Lines from Hal Summers, three songs for unaccompanied choir

Guitar studies (in collaboration with Richard Wright): *Advent Song; Beachcomber; Valentine; Grasshopper*

Duets for teacher & pupil guitar duo (in collaboration with Richard Wright): *Air; Best Foot Forward; Conversation Piece; Pastor Fido*

1998 Six Bagatelles (Set 1) for piano

Root and Branch, duetto for cello & double bass

Concertino, 'Les Dentelles', for two guitars & string orchestra

String Quartet No. 5

Bush Ballads (2nd series) for mid-range voice & piano

St Elmo's Fire for wind orchestra

Echoes of Autumn for viola & guitar

1999 *High Barbaree* for recorder, guitar & harpsichord

Piano Quintet No. 2

Concertino for flute, harp & string orchestra

2000 *Philip's Repose* for brass quintet

Essay No. 8 for orchestra

Diversions, five miniatures for wind quintet

Violin Sonata No. 1 for violin & piano

Concerto Chacony for treble recorder & string orchestra

Lighting the Match for double bass & piano

Piano Trio No. 3

Beyond Orion (extension to *Orion*, 1984) for clarinet quartet & brass quintet

2001 *Friends* for unaccompanied choir

String Quartet No. 6

Home-Bred Pictures, five songs for choir & harp

Cerberus for tuba & piano

2002 String Quartet No. 7, 'Cross-Currents'

Watersmeet for solo guitar & guitar ensemble

Warbeck Trio for recorder, bassoon & harpsichord

Concerto for trumpet & wind band

Venus to the Muses for soprano, recorder, bassoon & harpsichord

Trumpet Concerto with wind orchestra

2003 *Bush Ballads* (3rd series) for two voices (mezzo-soprano &
      baritone) & piano
      Piano Sonata No. 7
      Windbag, five occasional pieces for ten occasional players, for
      double wind quintet
      Quintet for flute & string quartet

2004 Duo for horn & harp
      Violin Sonata No. 2 for violin & piano
      The Monk and his Cat for soprano, recorder & piano
      Corobono for trombone choir
      The River God for choir & guitar

2005 String Quartet No. 8
      Sonata for trombone & chamber orchestra
      Six Bagatelles (Set 2) for piano
      Capriccio Concertante No. 2 for recorder, harpsichord &
      string orchestra
      Two Choral Songs for unaccompanied choir
      Roundelay for cello & guitar ensemble
      Jove's Nod for baritone, two violins, cello & harpsichord

2006 String Quartet No. 9
      Fancy Fair, three songs for baritone & piano quintet
      Régumar for recorder, guitar & marimba
      Far Away and Long Ago (in collaboration with Richard Wright)
      for guitar trio

2007 *Concert de Carillon* for two harpsichords & string quintet
      (amplified version of *Carillon*, 1967)
      Nancy the Waterman, chamber opera in one act, for four singers,
      violin, horn & piano
      Quintet for clarinet & string quartet

2008 *Two's Company*, suite for bassoon & cello
      Canticle of the Sun for unaccompanied choir
      Anne Hunter's Song for Eve for soprano & piano
      Five Minutes for wind quintet
      Two Romantic Pieces (Set B) for cello & piano

2009 *Wind in the Reeds* for oboe, clarinet & bassoon
     Riley & Co., four songs for baritone, recorder & guitar
2010 Essay No. 9 for orchestra
2011 Trumpet Concerto for trumpet & chamber orchestra

Recordings (Commercial Releases)

Opera

Margaret Catchpole: Two Worlds Apart
(Chamber opera in four acts)

Kate Howden (mezzo-soprano), William Wallace (tenor), Nicholas
Morris (bass), Alistair Ollerenshaw (baritone), Richard Edgar-Wilson
(tenor), Diana Moore (mezzo-soprano), Peter Willcock (bass), Matthew
Brook (bass), Julia Sporsén (soprano); Perpetuo / Julian Perkins
Naxos 8.660459-61 (3 discs) [2021]

Orchestral / Solo with Orchestra

Guitar Concertos

Guitar Concerto No. 1

John Williams (guitar); English Chamber Orchestra / Charles Groves
Sony G010003382789U [1968/2015]

Guitar Concertos

Guitar Concerto No. 2

John Williams (guitar); English Chamber Orchestra / Charles Groves
Sony G010003389356Y [1977/2015]

Stephen Dodgson: Concerto for Flute & Strings; Duo Concerto; Last of the Leaves
Concerto for flute & strings
Last of the Leaves
Duo Concerto for violin, guitar & strings
Michael George (bass-baritone), John Bradbury (clarinet), Jean-Jacques Kantorow (violin), Anthea Gifford (guitar); Northern Sinfonia / Ronald Zollman
Biddulph LAW 013 [1994]

Follow the Star
Concertino, 'Les Dentelles'
Riversong
Promenade I
Pastourelle
Follow the Star,
Eden Stell Guitar Duo: Mark Eden, Christopher Stell; Helen Sanderson (guitar); Orchestra Nova / George Vass
BGS CD 108 [2003]

English Music for Strings
Essay No. 7 for string orchestra
Royal Liverpool Philharmonic Orchestra / Martin Yates
Dutton Epoch CDLX 7244 [2010]

Essays for Orchestra
Essays Nos. 1–5
Royal Scottish National Orchestra / David Lloyd-Jones
Dutton Epoch CDLX 7236 [2010]

Choral

Deck the Hall: Songs for Christmas
Illuminare Jerusalem
The King's Singers: Nigel Perrin, Alastair Hume (countertenors), Alastair Thompson (tenor), Anthony Holt, Simon Carrington (baritones), Brian Kay (bass)
EMI Classics CDM 7 64133 2 [1973/1991]

Music for the Queen of Heaven: Contemporary Marian Motets
Dormi Jesu (from A Christmas Collection)
The Marian Consort / Rory McCleery
Delphian DCD 34190 [2017]

Canticle of the Sun
Canticle of the Sun
Four Poems of Mary Coleridge
'tis Almost One
Winter
Lullaby
All Bells in Paradise
Lines from Hal Summers
Katherine Bicknell (flute), Michael Higgins (organ); Sonoro / Neil Ferris
SOMM SOMMCD 0686 [2024]

Song

Songs for Voice and Guitar
Four Poems of John Clare for high voice & guitar
John Williams (guitar), Wilfred Brown (tenor)
Sony G010003383328X [1970/2015]

Songs of Freedom

Seven Songs of Federico Garcia Lorca
(words: Odissefs Elitis; music: Mikis Theodorakis, arr.:Stephen Dodgson)
Maria Farantouri (voice) & John Williams (guitar)
CBS S 72947 [1971]; Sony Classical SMK 62266 [1995]

Songs, Vol. 1: The Peasant Poet

Four Poems of John Clare
Mrs Hen
Heaven-Haven
Five Eyes
The Monk and his Cat
Bush Ballads (2nd series)
A Leaf in the River & Shrovetide Procession (from Eight Fanciful Pieces for piano)
Irishry
Tideways
Inversnaid
Slow, Slow, Fresh Fount
Ailish Tynan (soprano), Katie Bray (mezzo-soprano), James Gilchrist (tenor), Roderick Williams (baritone), Mark Eden (guitar), Ian Wilson (recorder), Christopher Glynn (piano)
SOMM SOMMCD 0659 [2022]

Songs, Vol. 2: The Distances Between

The Distances Between
Bagatelles (Set 1) for piano, Nos. 2–5
The Lamb
Song for Eve
Lachrymae
Bush Ballads (1st series)
The Sunflower
A Gypsy Prayer
Riley & Co.

Ailish Tynan (soprano), Katie Bray (mezzo-soprano), Marcus
Farnsworth (baritone), Mark Eden (guitar), Ian Wilson (recorder),
Christopher Glynn (piano)
SOMM SOMMCD 0673 [2023]

Songs, Vol. 3
Three Songs (to Words of TL Beddoes)
The Mower to the Glow-Worms
Winter Heavens
Daphne to Apollo
Il Zoppo and Mirage (from Eight Fanciful Pieces for piano)
Bush Ballads (3rd series)
The Stone
Turn Ye To Me
London Lyrics
Ailish Tynan (soprano), Katie Bray (mezzo-soprano), James Gilchrist
(tenor), Roderick Williams (baritone), Mark Eden (guitar), Christopher
Glynn (piano)
SOMM (catalogue number not yet known) [2025]

*See also the following recordings below: High Barbaree (Campion Cameo
CAMEO 2032); Guitar Chamber Works (Naxos 8.573762); Chamber Music,
Vol. 4: Music for Winds I (Toccata TOCC 0453 [2019]); Watersmeet
(Cadenza Music CACD 0603); Stephen Dodgson: Concerto for Flute &
Strings; Duo Concerto; Last of the Leaves (Biddulph LAW 013)*

Solo / duet / accompanied instrumental

Julian Bream – A Tribute, Vol. 2
Partita No. 1
Julian Bream (guitar)
Doremi DHR 8151/2 [recorded 1965, issued 2021]

Music for Guitar & Harpsichord
Duo Concertante for guitar & harpsichord
John Williams (guitar), Rafael Puyana (harpsichord)
Sony G010003383390N [1972/2015]

Guitar Music from England, Japan, Brazil, Venezuela, Argentina and Mexico
Fantasy-Divisions for guitar
John Williams (guitar)
Sony G0100033841995 [1973/2015]

Piano Sonatas, Vol. 1
Piano Sonatas Nos. 2, 4 & 5
Bernard Roberts (piano)
Claudio CC 4431-2 [1994/2019]

Piano Sonatas, Vol. 2
Piano Sonatas Nos. 1, 3 & 6
Bernard Roberts (piano)
Claudio CC 4941-2 [1999/2019]

Amadeus Guitar Duo play ...
Pastourelle
Amadeus Guitar Duo: Dale Kavanagh, Thomas Kirchhoff (guitars)
Hänssler CD 98.338 [1999]

Beyond the Dark
Duo for flute & harp
Anna Noakes (flute), Gillian Tingay (harp)
Guild GMCD 7202 [2000]

Dialogues – The Music of Stephen Dodgson, Vol. 2
Dialogues for guitar & harpsichord
The Troubled Midnight
Suites Nos. 1 & 2 for clavichord
Sketchbook for two lutes
Roberto Morón Pérez (guitar), Julian Perkins (clavichord), Pawel
Siwczak (harpsichord), Elizabeth Kenny (lute), Jacob Heringman (lute)
Campion Cameo CAMEO 2088 [2009]

Music for an Island
Promenade for two guitars
Eden Stell Guitar Duo: Mark Eden, Christopher Stell (guitars)
BGS CD 117 [2009]

Solo
Cor Leonis
J Bernardo Silva (horn)
Afinaudio IRFC.08.140 [2010]

Dances with Harpsichords
Tambourin (from Suite No. 1 for Clavichord)
Elaine Funaro (harpsichord)
Centaur CRC 2651 [2014]

Guitar Recital: Eren Süalp
Partita No. 1
Eren Süalp (guitar)
Naxos 8.573487 [2015]

Panorama 1919–2013: A Century of British Keyboard Music
Inventions, Set 2, Nos. 5 & 6
Penelope Cave (harpsichord)
Prima Facie PFCD 048 [2016]

Chamber Music, Vol. 1: Complete Music for Cello and Piano
Two Romantic Pieces (Sets A & B)
Sonata for cello & piano
Five Occasional Pieces
Evva Mizerska (cello), Emma Abbate (piano)
Toccata TOCC 0353 [2016]

Easy Studies For Guitar, Vol. 2
12 Transitional Studies
Cristiano Porqueddu (guitar)
Brilliant Classics 95557 [2017]

24 Inventions for Harpsichord
Inventions, Sets 1–4
Ekaterina Likhina (harpsichord)
Naxos 9.70262 [2017]

Colloquy: Works for Guitar Duo
Promenade I
Duo Guitartes: Anne-Kathrin Gerbeth, Bernhard Dolch (guitars)
EM Records EMRCD 067 [2021]

This Curious Harp: 20th-Century British Music for Solo Harp
Ballade
Fantasy
Eleanor Hudson (harp)
Willowhayne Records MPR 110 [2021]

Sarabanda for Merlin: Guitar Works of Stephen Dodgson
Partitas Nos. 1 & 2
Fantasy-Divisions
Legend
Merlin
The Midst of Life
Paolo Spadetto (guitar)
Rainbow Classics RW201990971-77 [2022]

Tournament for Twenty Fingers
Tournament for Twenty Fingers
Sonata for piano duet
Emma Abbate, Julian Perkins (piano four hands)
BIS 2578 [2022]

Inventions: Contemporary Music for Harpsichord, Vol. 2
Sonata-Divisions
Inventions, Set 5
Katarzyna Kowalik (harpsichord)
Prima Facie PFCD 195 [2023]

Mirage: Piano Music By Stephen Dodgson
Eight Fanciful Pieces
Four Moods of the Wind
Three Impromptus
Piano Sonata No. 7
Six Bagatelles (Set 2)
Rondo in Ab (download only)
Osman Tack (piano)
SOMM SOMMCD 0684 [2024]

See also the following recordings listed in this section: High Barbaree
(Campion Cameo CAMEO 2032); The Peasant Poet (SOMM SOMMCD
0659); The Distances Between (SOMM SOMMCD 0673); String Trios
(Naxos 8.573856); Watersmeet (Cadenza Music CACD 0603)

Chamber

Just Brass
Suite for Brass Septet
Philip Jones Brass Ensemble
Argo/Decca ZRG 655 [1970/2018]

Sonata for Brass Quintet
Philip Jones Brass Ensemble
Lyrita SRCD 307 [1975/2008]

Noël
Schütz: Die Weisen aus dem Morgenlande (arr.)
Lord Jesus Hath A Garden (arr.)
God Rest Ye Merry Gentlemen (arr.)
Philip Jones Brass Ensemble
Decca SXDL 7576 [1982]

Diamonds
Five Penny Pieces
Lyadov: Eight Russian Folksongs
Harlequin: Mark Underwood (flute, piccolo), Bryony Otaki (oboe),
Graeme Vinall (clarinet), James Thomson (horn), Glyn Williams (bassoon)
Chromattica 0800 [2000]

Piano Trios & Bagatelles
Piano Trios Nos. 1–3
Bagatelles (Set 1) for piano
Bernard Roberts Piano Trio: Bernard Roberts (piano), Andrew Roberts
(violin), Nicholas Roberts (cello)
Claudio CC 5257-2 [2002/2019]

High Barbaree – The Music of Stephen Dodgson
High Barbaree
Venus to the Muses
Daphne to Apollo
Duo Concertante
Shine and Shade
Quatre Rondeaux de Charles d'Orléans
Inventions for harpsichord, Set 3, Nos. 1, 3, 4 & 6
Warbeck Trio

Lesley-Jane Rogers (soprano), John Turner (recorder), Graham Salvage
(bassoon), Craig Ogden (guitar), Pamela Nash (harpsichord)
Campion Cameo CAMEO 2032 [2004]

Jolly Boating Weather – Music from Eton

Scarlatti: Sonata Kk 394 (arr.)
Eton College Brass Ensemble
Herald HAVPCD 320 [2006]

Watersmeet: The Music of Stephen Dodgson (Chamber Music with Guitar)

Watersmeet
London Lyrics
Partita No. 4
Duo for cello & guitar
Personent Hodie
Jonathan Leathwood (guitar), Neil Jenkins (tenor), Rohan de Saram
(cello); TETRA Guitar Quartet: Stephen Goss, Richard Hand, Graham
Roberts, Bridget Upson; Aquarelle Guitar Quartet: Michael Baker,
Vasilis Bessas, James Jervis, Richard Sathill; Appassionata Guitar Trio:
Rebecca Baulch, Amanda Cook, Hayley Savage; Carl Herring (guitar)
Cadenza Music CACD 0603 [2006]

String Quartets, Vol. 1

String Quartets Nos. 1, 5, 6 & 7
Tippett Quartet: John Mills, Jeremy Isaac (violins), Maxime Moore
(viola), Bozidar Vukotic (cello)
Dutton Epoch CDLX 7182 [2007]

String Quartets, Vol. 2

String Quartets Nos. 3 & 4
Quintet for guitar & string quartet
Tippett Quartet: John Mills, Jeremy Isaac (violins), Maxime Moore
(viola), Bozidar Vukotic (cello); Craig Ogden (guitar)
Dutton Epoch CDLX 7214 [2008]

String Quartets, Vol. 3
String Quartets Nos. 2, 8 & 9
String Sextet
Quintet for flute & string quartet
Quintet for clarinet & string quartet
Tippett Quartet: John Mills, Jeremy Isaac (violins), Maxime Moore/Julia
O'Riordan (viola), Bozidar Vukotic (cello); John Bradbury (clarinet),
Robert Stallman (flute), Julia O'Riordan (viola), Caroline Dale (cello)
Dutton Epoch CDLX 7265 (2 discs) [2011]

English Music for Oboe
Oboe Quartet
Sarah Francis (oboe), Tagore String Trio: Frances Mason (violin), Brian
Schiele (viola), James Halsey (cello)
Heritage HTGCD 275 [2014]

The Leaves Be Green
Intermezzo (Citharae Chordae pro Pace) for four guitars
VIDA Guitar Quartet: Mark Ashford, Amanda Cook, Mark Eden,
Christopher Stell (guitars)
BGS CD 126 [2015]

Chamber Music, Vol. 2: Three Quintets
Piano Quintets Nos. 1 & 2
String Quintet
Tippett Quartet: : John Mills, Jeremy Isaac (violins), Lydia Lowndes-
Northcott (viola), Bozidar Vukotic (cello); Emma Abbate (piano),
Susan Monks (cello)
Toccata TOCC 0357 [2017]

Guitar Chamber Works

Change-Ringers
Roundelay
Divertissement
Intermezzo (Citharae Chordae pro Pace)
Hymnus de Sancto Stephano
Four Poems of John Clare
The Selevan Story
Antonia Gentile (soprano), Octavia Lamb (flute), Hartmut Richter
(violin), Evva Mizerska (cello), Michael Butten (octave bass guitar),
Eden Stell Guitar Duo, Mēla Guitar Quartet: Matthew Robinson,
George Tarlton, Daniel Bovey, Jiva Housden
Naxos 8.573762 [2017]

Chamber Music, Vol. 3: Music for Oboe

Sonata for oboe & piano
Countdown
Sonata for cor anglais & piano
Three Winter Songs
Suite in C minor
James Turnbull (oboe), Libby Burgess (piano), Eleanor Turner (harp),
Robyn Allegra Parton (soprano)
Toccata TOCC 0444 [2017]

Chamber Music with Harp and Guitar

Septet Variations
Pastoral Sonata
Solway Suite
Echoes of Autumn
Sonata for Three
Capriccio and Finale
Karolos: Juliette Bausor (flute), Maximiliano Martin (clarinet), Harriet
Mackenzie (violin), Philippa Mo (violin), Sarah-Jane Bradley (viola),
Graham Walker (cello), Craig Ogden (guitar), Tanya Houghton (harp)
Naxos 8.573857 [2018]

String Trios

String Trios Nos. 1 & 2
Sonatina in B minor
Caprice after Puck
Partita for solo cello
Karolos: Harriet Mackenzie (violin), Sarah-Jane Bradley (viola),
Graham Walker (cello)
Naxos 8.573856 [2018]

Chamber Music, Vol. 4: Music for Winds I

Sonata for wind quintet
Gipsy Songs
Wind in the Reeds
Sonata for horn & piano
Trio for oboe, bassoon & piano
Five Minutes for wind quintet
Kate Howden (mezzo-soprano), Magnard Ensemble: Suzannah
Clements (flute), Mana Shibata (oboe), Joseph Shiner (clarinet). Catriona
McDermid (bassoon), Jonathan Farey (horn), Suling King (piano)
Toccata TOCC 0453 [2019]

Chamber Music, Vol. 5: Music for Winds II

Quintet for piano & wind quartet
Serenade for oboe, clarinet & bassoon
Baermann's Treasure
Baermann – The Sequel
Suite for wind quintet
Duo for horn & harp
Promenade II for wind quintet
Magnard Ensemble: Suzannah Clements (flute), Mana Shibata (oboe),
Joseph Shiner (clarinet). Catriona McDermid (bassoon), Jonathan
Farey (horn), Suling King (piano); Olivia Jageurs (harp)
Toccata TOCC 0499 [2020]

Recordings (Trust Archive)

Live recordings and radio broadcasts in the Stephen Dodgson Charitable Trust collection
(Dates and other information provided where known)

Orchestral / Solo with Orchestra

Guitar Concertos 1 and 2 – John Williams (guitar); English Chamber Orchestra / Charles Groves

Piano Concerto – Frieda Valenzi (piano); Vienna Symphony Orchestra / Armando Aliberti (1960)

Concerto da Camera No. 2 for flute, clarinet & string orchestra (1966)

Concerto da Camera No. 4 for piano & string orchestra – Thomas McIntosh Philomusica (1971)

Concerto da Camera No. 3 for two flutes, violin & string orchestra – Mary Ryan, Patricia Linden (flutes), Trevor Williams (violin); Tilford Bach Orchestra / Denys Darlow (1973)

Bassoon Concerto – Martin Gatt (bassoon); English Chamber Orchestra / Frederik Prausnitz (1977)

Sinfonia: Troia Nova – St Paul's School Chamber Orchestra (1990)

Symphony in One Movement – Royal Academy of Music Chamber Orchestra / Stephen Dodgson (1990)

Wind and Brass Orchestras and Ensembles

Suite for brass septet – Philip Jones Brass Ensemble (1957)
Epigrams from a Garden – Pamela Bowden (contralto); National Youth Wind Orchestra / Harry Legge (1977)
The Eagle – National Wind Band of Scotland / Rodney Bashford (1982)
Wind Symphony – National Youth Wind Orchestra / Harry Legge (1985)
Arlington Concertante – Linton Powell (harpsichord); University of Texas Wind Ensemble / Ray Lichtenwalter (1987)
A Galliard Ground (Inglott arr. Dodgson) – Royal Academy of Music Student Brass Ensemble (1990)
Orion Nonet – Royal Academy of Music clarinet and brass student ensemble (1990)
Matelot (after Grieg's Sailor's Song) – National Youth Wind Orchestra / Adrian Brown (1990)
Capriccio Concertante – Royal Northern College of Music Wind Orchestra / Andrew Smith (1990)
The Flowers of London Town – University of Kansas Symphonic Wind Band / Robert Foster (1991)
Bandwagon – National Youth Wind Orchestra / Adrian Brown (1993)
Partita for Ten Wind Instruments – National Youth Wind Orchestra Chamber Ensemble (1995)
St Elmo's Fire – Royal Northern College of Music Wind Orchestra / James Gourlay (2001)

Choral Music

The Soul's Progress – Eileen McLoughlin, Nancy Thomas (soloists); BBC Chorus, Brass Ensemble of LPO / Leslie Woodgate (1957)
Hymn to Harmony – Badminton School Choir & Orchestra
Te Deum – Tilford Bach Festival Choir & Orchestra / Denys Darlow (1973)
Magnificat – Tilford Bach Festival Choir & Orchestra / Denys Darlow (1975)

'Tis Almost One – Choir of King's College Cambridge / Stephen Cleobury (1986)

Sir John – Michael Bochman (violin), Jonathan Williams (horn), Caroline Palmer (piano); BBC Northern Singers / Stephen Wilkinson (1987)

The Innocents – BBC Northern Singers / Stephen Wilkinson (1989)

The Country Wedding – Sarah Hydes (violin); Felling Male Voice Choir / Stephen Dodgson (1995)

The River God – John MacKenzie (guitar); Chanticleer Singers / Jane Sturmheit (2005)

Invocation, Lullaby, Winter, All Bells in Paradise and 'Echoing Carol' from *A Christmas Collection* – Peregrine Ensemble / Daniel Collins (2023)

Four Poems of Mary Coleridge – Carla Finesilver (flute); Pegasus / Matthew Altham (2023)

Home-Bred Pictures – Esther Beyer (harp); Barnes Festival Consort / James Day (2023)

Two Choral Songs – Pegasus, Peregrine Ensemble and Barnes Festival Consort / James Day (2023)

Vocal Music – Opera and Solo

Gipsy Songs – Alison Truefitt (mezzo-soprano), Julia Rayson (clarinet), Alan Schiller (piano)

John Clare's Wooing Songs – Hilliard Ensemble, Lena-Liis Kiessel (piano)

Epigrams from a Garden – Pamela Bowden (contralto); National Youth Wind Orchestra / Harry Legge (1977)

Cadilly – Christine Page, Rosemary Jensen, Peter Kestner, Andrew Gallagher (soloists); unnamed wind quintet / Keith Swanwick (1979)

The Tower – Mark Rowlinson (baritone), Stephen Cleobury (organ) (1984)

Riley & Co. – Terence Ayebare (baritone), John Turner (recorder), Craig Ogden (guitar)

Instrumental Solo and Chamber Music

String Trio No. 1 – Neville Marriner (violin), Stephen Shingles (viola),
Alexander Kok (cello) (1953)

Duo for flute & harp – Maria Korchinska (flute), Geoffrey Gilbert
(harp) (1954)

Six Inventions, Set 1 – Stanislav Heller (1956)

Suite in C minor – Tony Danby (oboe), Geoffrey Connah (piano) (1957)

Serenade for oboe, clarinet & bassoon – London Reed Trio (1960)

String Trio No. 2 – The Esterhazy Trio: Brenda Cullity (violin), Ruth
David (viola), Daphne Webb (cello) (1964)

Five Occasional Pieces for cello & piano – Rohan de Saram (cello),
Druvi de Saram (piano) (1974)

Trio for baryton, viola & cello – Riki Gerardy (baryton), Czaba Erdely
(viola), Jonathan Williams (cello) (1976)

Capriccio after Puck – Czaba Erdely (viola) (1976)

Sonata for Wind Quintet – Vienna Wind Quintet (1978)

In Search of Folly – Frank Nagel Walter Feybli (1986)

Five Occasional Pieces for violin & piano – Frances Mason (violin),
Michael Freyhan (piano) (1985)

Partita for solo cello – Rohan de Saram (1988)

Sonata for oboe & piano – David Wilson (oboe), Alvin Moisey
(piano) (1987)

Baermann's Treasure – Thea King (clarinet), Clifford Benson (piano) (1989)

Five Occasional Pieces for flute & piano – Robert Stallman (flute),
Kiyoshi Tamagawa (piano) (1990)

Pastoral Sonata for flute, cello & guitar – Trio Mondrian (1990)

Bagatelles for four clarinets – Thurston Clarinet Quartet (1992)

Solitaire – Simon Hogg (trombone) (1993)

Echoes of Autumn – Francesco Venga (viola), Duilio Meucci (guitar) (2011)

Sonata for Three – Nicola Smedley (flute), Isabel Pereira (viola),
Thomas Lavigne (guitar) (2004)

Partita for solo cello – Kieran Carter (2019)

Duo for cello and guitar – Kieran Carter (cello), Dan Bovey (guitar) (2019)

Contributors

Lance Bosman is a guitarist, music editor, composer, and writer on music. Between 1972 and 1992 he conducted interviews with many leading composers, including Hans Werner Henze, Malcolm Arnold and Lennox Berkeley, for the journal *Guitar International* (these can all be read at https://www.lancebosman. co.uk). He is the author of *Harmony for Guitar*, which introduces students to both traditional and modern idioms, and he is currently working on a book project titled *Music for Guitar, Lute and Vihuela Through the Ages*, which covers the plucked repertory from the 16th century to the present day. His compositions for solo guitar have recently been recorded by the Finnish guitarist Janne Malinen (2022).

Joanna Bullivant is Lecturer in Music at the Royal Birmingham Conservatoire, having previously worked at the University of Oxford, University of Nottingham and King's College London. Her research centres on 19th- and 20th-century British music, particularly musical and cultural histories of minority groups. Her first monograph, *Alan Bush, Modern Music and the Cold War: The Cultural Left in Britain and the Communist Bloc* was published by Cambridge University Press in 2017. This was based on a decade of research into the musical culture of British communism and its relationship to wider British and communist politics and culture.

More recently, Jo has been engaged in studying digital methods of understanding composers' compositional processes and disseminating that knowledge to wider audiences. She pursued this in several projects at Oxford University, including the AHRC-funded *Delius, Modernism and the Sound of Place* (2015–16), *Digital Delius* (2017–18), *The Dream of Gerontius: Curating Catholic Music Digitally* (2019–21) and *Diversity and the British String Quartet* (2020). Through these activities Jo created the Delius Catalogue of Works, which won the British Library Labs Research Award in 2018. She has also curated and written content on Delius and Elgar for the British Library's flagship digital music resource Discovering Music, and collaborated with the British Library, the National Trust, and the US National Institute for Newman Studies (NINS) on a project digitising and interpreting the original manuscript of Elgar's *The Dream of Gerontius*. Following a Visiting Fellowship at NINS, she is now embarking on a second monograph project entitled *Elgar and the Catholic Imagination*.

Oliver Chandler is Director of Studies in Music at Hertford and Keble Colleges, University of Oxford; he is also an academic professor at the Royal College of Music. He has co-written two books, *Return to Riemann: Tonal Function and Chromatic Music* (RMA Monographs) and *A Twelve-Tone Repertory for Guitar: Julian Bream and the British Serialists, 1956-1983* (GFA Monographs), and he has published on a number of other music-theoretical topics in major academic journals, including *Music Analysis, Music & Letters* and *Music Theory Online*. A keen guitarist, he was awarded the guitar-departmental prize by Trinity Laban in 2015.

Phillip Cooke is active as both a composer and musicologist, working with many of the leading choirs and ensembles in the

UK and further afield. His work has regularly been premiered and broadcast on BBC Radio 3 and has also been broadcast on BBC Radio 4, Classic FM and many international broadcasters. There are currently 15 commercial recordings available featuring his music. He is strongly influenced by his native Lake District and by history. His main musical influences are found in continuing and reconciling a pastoral British tradition; he has written articles on Edward Elgar and Herbert Howells and contemporary British composers including Francis Pott, Cecilia McDowall and Judith Bingham. He co-edited a book of essays on Howells which was published by Boydell and Brewer in October 2013 and wrote the first major study on James MacMillan's music that was published by the same publishers in June 2019. In 2007–08 he was a Career Development Fellow at the Faculty of Music, Oxford University, and a Junior Research Fellow (2007–10) at The Queen's College, Oxford University. He was composition tutor at Eton College in 2011–12. In January 2013 he was appointed a Lecturer in Composition at Aberdeen University, becoming Deputy Head in 2015, Senior Lecturer in 2017 and was Head of Music from 2018 to 2021. He became Professor of Composition in July 2022.

Simon Ferris read music and was organ scholar at King's College, London. As an undergraduate he pursued additional instrumental and musicianship studies with Bernard Oram at the Guildhall School of Music and Drama and, after graduation, received composition tuition and encouragement from the composer and John Ireland pupil, Geoffrey Bush.

Simon works as a pianist, composer, arranger, writer, conductor and teacher. His professional experience ranges from appearing as a classical piano recitalist, to working as a jazz pianist playing at the Cork International Jazz Festival and onstage in London's West End; from preparing children's choirs for the Royal Opera House, Covent Garden, to conducting symphonies by Mahler and Shostakovich. He is the composer of an extensive catalogue of choral and educational music, the author of a biography of Beethoven (Omnibus Press, 2018), and an educational specialist working on the specification and exam setting panel for Cambridge Assessment.

Simon is the founder-director of the Thames Youth Orchestra and Director of Music at The Henrietta Barnett School, having been for many years Composer in Residence at Tiffin School, and Musician in Residence at The Tiffin Girls' School, Kingston upon Thames

Thomas Hyde is a composer based in London. His output includes the one-man opera, *That Man Stephen Ward*, released commercially on Resonus Classics, a string quartet, a Symphony for the BBC Scottish Symphony Orchestra, and a comedy overture based on Les Dawson premiered by the BBC National Orchestra of Wales and Dalia Stasevska. He is a member of the music department at King's College London, and in 2019 was elected to a Senior Research Fellowship at Worcester College, Oxford. He is chair of the Lucille Graham Trust, a Vice President of the Presteigne Festival and an Associate of the Royal Academy of Music. He has just completed a full-length opera, *Aiding and Abetting*, to a libretto by Sir Alexander McCall Smith (after the novel by Muriel Spark), commissioned by Scottish Opera.

Stuart O'Hara is a London-based bass-baritone. He divides his time between the Choir of Westminster Abbey, where he is a lay vicar, and freelance career based on a healthy mix of choral, consort and solo work. He regularly performs and records with I Fagiolini, The Carice Singers, London Choral Sinfonia,

Ensemble Pro Victoria and Armonico Consort. As a soloist, he particularly enjoys singing the music of JS Bach, *Lieder* and Russian song.

He studied for a Master's in Solo Voice Ensemble Singing under the tutelage of Robert Hollingworth at the University of York, and regularly returns to his alma mater to work with students, including a fruitful partnership with Cypriot pianist Ioanna Koullepou exploring the ballads of Carl Loewe, Romantic performance practice, and the evolution of the early piano. He maintains a good relationship with York Late Music's recital series, through which he has explored late 20th- and 21st-century English song, regularly premiering new repertoire by Yorkshire poets and composers.

He wrote for the Merseyside music magazine *Bido Lito!* for seven years, during which time he covered contemporary classical and social topics, interviewing members of Manchester Collective and Conductor Laureate of the Royal Liverpool Philharmonic Orchestra, Vasily Petrenko.

Robert Matthew-Walker studied at Goldsmiths College, and (now) University of the Arts, London. After leaving the Army in 1962, he studied with Darius Milhaud in Paris in 1962–63.

He founded the Tunnel Club rock venue in Greenwich, joining CBS Records in 1970, becoming Director of Masterworks Europe. Later joining RCA Records, he launched James Galway's solo career, won the Grand Prix du Disque for his RCA recording of Brian Ferneyhough's *Sonatas for String Quartet*, and also appeared with the rapper Adamski on a dance single, *Kraktali Daze*.

Robert Matthew-Walker later edited *Music and Musicians*, and has been editor of *Musical Opinion* and *The Organ* since 2008. He has published 24 books, including four books on Edvard Grieg, the fights of Muhammad Ali, and five books on rock music, among them a biography of Madonna and two studies of Elvis Presley. He has also been a Fellow of the Atlantic Council of Great Britain. His compositions include six symphonies (1956–68), *Symphonic Variations* for orchestra, seven concertos, seven string quartets and various violin and four piano sonatas. Commercial recordings of Robert Matthew-Walker's music have been issued on the Naxos, Guild, SOMM and Toccata Classics labels.

Pamela Nash was introduced to the harpsichord whilst a student of Heather Slade-Lipkin at Chetham's School of Music in Manchester. She went on to study with Valda Aveling at Trinity College of Music in London, where she was awarded the Raymond Russell Harpsichord Prize, and later with Huguette Dreyfus at the Schola Cantorum in Paris. As a Harkness Fellow, she gained a Master of Music degree in Early Keyboard Instruments at the University of Michigan, studying with Edward Parmentier.

Having developed an interest in the work of living composers, Pamela went on to direct the Manchester new music festivals Harpsichordfest 2004 and 2006, as well as the British Harpsichord Society's International Composition Competition in 2013.

She has premiered works for solo and duo harpsichords by composers including Graham Fitkin, Gary Carpenter and Kevin Malone, and was producer for *Shadow Journey*, a CD of new harpsichord music on the Prima Facie label. She has contributed articles for *Contemporary Music Review*, *Sounding Board*, *Harpsichord & Fortepiano* and *The Diapason*, and was editor, in close collaboration with the composer, of the complete solo harpsichord sheet music of Stephen Dodgson which has now received a second publication by the Stephen Dodgson Charitable Trust.

Recent projects as Artistic Director include the bicentenary commemorations for Charlotte and Anne Brontë in Manchester, for which she commissioned poetry and choral works. She is a contributor to Vision Edition's book on the contemporary harpsichord, for publication in 2024.

Pamela maintains a thriving teaching practice and is harpsichord tutor at the University of Liverpool.

David Wordsworth studied at Leeds University, the City University (London) and the Guildhall, before working as a teacher and in music publishing for several years. More recently he has devoted himself to a full-time professional musical career. He was Music Director of the Addison Singers between 1995 and 2022. His choirs had a regular London season and toured many parts of Europe, also appearing at Carnegie Hall, New York, as well as at many UK festivals. David has conducted/adjudicated in Hungary, Poland, Ireland, Italy, Spain, France, Austria, Norway, Mexico, Cuba, the Philippines, and has held residencies at several universities in the USA. In 2016 he conducted the Marian Consort and the Berkeley Ensemble in a revival of Lennox Berkeley's *Stabat Mater*, performing at the Aldeburgh Easter, Spitalfields and Cheltenham Festivals, subsequently broadcasting the work for the BBC and recording it for Delphian Records. In 2018 David curated a year-long festival of American music at St John's, Smith Square, in London, where he appeared as both pianist and conductor. David's most recent performances have included a concert of English music at St Stephen's Cathedral, Vienna, and the premiere of a major choral/orchestral work by Judith Weir, as part of his last concert with The Addison Singers. His book *Giving Voice to my Music*, based on conversations with 24 choral composers, was published by Kahn & Averill in 2021. He is co-editor of and a contributor to *Gavin Bryars*, published by Kahn & Averill in 2023 to celebrate the composer's 80th birthday.

Image Credits

Photos of Stephen Dodgson composing, at piano, with Ronald Field, in the Fenlands, original cast of *Margaret Catchpole*, Bernard Roberts Trio and Bernard Roberts Thames-side walk © Robert Carpenter-Turner.

Photo of *Four Poems of Mary Coleridge* performance at Barnes Music Festival © Ben Tomlin.

Margaret Catchpole 2019 poster designed by Leonora Dawson-Bowling.

Prussia Cove photos courtesy of Stephen Gordon.

Barnes house images courtesy of Leonora Dawson-Bowling.

John Dodgson CD cover images courtesy of Naxos.

Eden Stell Guitar Duo photo courtesy of Mark Eden.

Swiss mountain photos with Philip and Ursula Jones courtesy of Ursula Jones.

Tippett Quartet photo courtesy of the Barnes Music Festival.

Imogen Whitehead photo courtesy of Imogen Whitehead.

All other photos courtesy of the Dodgson, Pease and Harvey families.

Index A – General

Note: Page numbers in *italic* denote images. Page numbers in the form 6n indicate a footnote.

Index B – Works

WORKS (by instrument/type)

brass

choral music